Ben Stacy Jerrik (Ed.)

Allakhazam

Ben Stacy Jerrik (Ed.)

Allakhazam

Massively multiplayer online role-playing game, EverQuest, Warhammer Online: Age of Reckoning

Part Press

Imprint

Publisher:
Part Press is a trademark of
International Book Market Service Ltd., 17 Rue Meldrum, Beau Bassin, 1713-01 Mauritius
Email: info@bookmarketservice.com
Website: www.bookmarketservice.com

Published in 2013

Printed in: U.S.A., U.K., Germany. This book was not produced in Mauritius.

ISBN: 978-620-1-60661-6

Contents

Articles

References

Allakhazam

Allakhazam's Magical Realm, part of the Zam Network, is a website providing forums, a wikibase and lookup services for several online RPGs, including *Aion*, Dark Age of Camelot, *EVE Online*, *EverQuest*, *EverQuest II*, *Final Fantasy XI*, *Free Realms*, *Lord of the Rings Online*, *Runes of Magic*, *Star Wars Galaxies*, *Warhammer Online*, and *World of Warcraft*.

As of December 7, 2008 it has over 1.4 million registered usernames and over 10 million posts between the forums and individual pages for each item in every game covered on the site.

The site's primary purpose is to enable registered users to search a range of databases relating to specific MMORPGs. These contain details of Quests, NPCs and in-game items, as well as interactive maps and advice on game-play. As the site developed a significant user-base, the interactive nature of the discussion allowed users to post comments on the various database items, thus ensuring the content and advice to gamers was current.

In addition to these databases, registered users can also download content to enable offline review of their current game characters, game patches and other gaming resources.

In recent years, the discussion forums have become an increasingly important feature of the site, with specific forums dedicated to each of the supported games, and more generalist areas such as Technical Support and Out of Topic discussions (for non-game related discussion).

History

Allakhazam.com was started in 1999 by Jeffrey Moyer as a simple guide to the game *EverQuest* on a free web hosting service. It quickly became known by the *EverQuest* player base for its extensive quest descriptions. Mr. Moyer then teamed up with programmer Andy Sharp, acquired the url allakhazam.com, and the site was expanded into a database format covering quests, items, mobs and other aspects of the game. By the year 2000, Allakhazam was the most popular site on the internet covering Everquest and was getting over 10 million page views a month. Many consider Allakhazam to be the innovator of the gaming database format that is now followed by a number of other networks.

In late 2000, the internet experienced a vast reduction of advertising revenue that has been referred to as the Dot-com bubble. Most gaming sites, including Allakhazam, lost the majority of their revenue. Many popular gaming sites went out of business soon thereafter and have not been seen since. Allakhazam weathered this storm by establishing a premium membership service where users paid for certain advanced searches and other features designed to make their game play easier. At its peak, the Allakhazam premium service had over 45,000 subscribers, making it one of the more successful services of its kind ever.

The success of *EverQuest* inspired other publishers to release their own online role playing games. As new games were released, Allakhazam added sites for them. Each Allakhazam site was popular with the gaming communities of the individual games. The release of Final Fantasy XI, however, was of particular note. Because publisher Square Enix did not launch its own official forums for the game, the Allakhazam FFXI forums became the main forums for that game. This led to a significant expansion of the entire Allakhazam forum system.

The launch of *World of Warcraft* in 2004 marked another significant milestone. Allakhazam launched an extensive database for the game that currently accounts for approximately 90% of their traffic. Allakhazam is regularly referred to as a reference for WoW information, and is particularly known for its quest descriptions and auction house information.

In February 2006, co-owners Moyer and Sharp sold their ownership stake in Allakhazam to Affinity Media Corporation. The amount of the sale has been said to be between 7 and 10 million dollars. Affinity Media created the Zam Network and consolidated Allakhazam with Thottbot and MMO Interface into the Internet's largest MMO Gaming information network. Later Zam also acquired Wowhead. Allakhazam, Thottbot and Wowhead are all ranked within the top 1,000 sites according to Alexa, and the combined traffic of these sites likely puts the Zam Network as one of the internet's top 100 sites in terms of total traffic. Indeed, the Zam Media Kit claims a total of over 700 million page views a month. Both Moyer and Sharp continued to work for the new corporation, and in 2008, Mr. Moyer was named as the president of the entire Zam network.

26 September 2009 Moyer via his Twitter Account announced he was leaving at the end of the month [1] "Yes it is true. Illia [Sharp] got fired a month ago and I am leaving Allakhazam at the end of this month. So sorry to see it end this way."

Unique site features

Premium vs regular registration

In order to access content and participate in the community, users must register an account. This is at no cost, all content is free to access. However some search features are restricted to Premium Users, who pay a subscription fee (currently ranging from $2.50 to $3.33 per month depending on the duration of subscription).

In addition, premium users can include a user image (or 'avatar') to their posts, use graphical emoticons or 'smilies' in the Forums, and access advanced search and support features.

Custom titles

On attaining 10,000 individual posts, a custom title is awarded by the Administrators; usually sarcastically based upon that user's posting style. This is in contrast to most other forums, where either a custom title can be set initially, or doesn't exist in the first place. As of September 22, 2008, fifty-six users have custom titles.

Karma system

While the site's forums and comments are watched by the site's administrators, a degree of control similar to, but more extensive than, Slashdot's is granted to a portion of the users by way of the karma system. In essence, posts can be rated up (increasing the poster's karma) or down (decreasing it) to manipulate whether or not the post meets the current filter criteria. Resulting posts that are "pushed under the filter (sub-default)" are invisible under the default settings on the forums. Unlike Slashdot's karma system, however, only a flat number is assigned to the posts and comments, rather than both a number and a type of rating.

Denial-of-service attacks

According to a statement on the site's home page,[2] on February 21, 2008 the Allakhazam site became a victim of a denial-of-service attack in an attempt to block users from accessing the site. This recurred on March 3, 2008 as the site became inaccessible to users, forcing the site's owners to change their service provider.[3] Normal service was restored on March 5, 2008, but another denial-of-service attack took down the site again on March 11, 2008. New hardware was added to compensate for this continual attack, and the site has not experienced any major downtimes since then.

References

[1] Moyers Twitter (http://twitter.com/Allakhazam1/status/4387958566)
[2] Allakhazam.com: News - DDOS Attack (http://www.allakhazam.com/sdetail.html?story=12388)
[3] Allakhazam.com: News - We're Back (http://www.allakhazam.com/sdetail.html?story=12500)

External links

- Allakhazam (http://www.allakhazam.com/)

Massively_multiplayer_online_role-playing_game

Massively multiplayer online role-playing game (**MMORPG**) is a genre of role-playing video games or web browser based games in which a very large number of players interact with one another within a virtual game world.

As in all RPGs, players assume the role of a character (often in a fantasy world or science-fiction world) and take control over many of that character's actions. MMORPGs are distinguished from single-player or small multi-player online RPGs by the number of players, and by the game's persistent world (usually hosted by the game's publisher), which continues to exist and evolve while the player is offline and away from the game.

MMORPGs are played throughout the world. Worldwide revenues for MMORPGs exceeded half a billion dollars in 2005,[] and Western revenues exceeded US$1 billion in 2006.[1] In 2008, Western consumer spending on subscription MMOGs grew to $1.4 billion.[2] *World of Warcraft*, a popular MMORPG, has more than 8 million subscribers as of March 2013.[] *Star Wars: The Old Republic*, released in 2011, became the world's 'Fastest-Growing MMO Ever' after gaining 1 million subscribers within the first three days of its launch.[3] [4]

Common features

Although modern MMORPGs sometimes differ dramatically from their antecedents, many of them share some basic characteristics. These include several common features: persistent game environment, some form of progression, social interaction within the game, in-game culture, system architecture, membership in a group, and character customization.

Themes

The majority of popular MMORPGs are based on traditional fantasy themes, often occurring in an in-game universe comparable to that of *Dungeons & Dragons*. Some employ hybrid themes that either merge or substitute fantasy elements with those of science fiction, sword and sorcery, or crime fiction. Still others draw thematic material from American comic books, the occult, and other genres. Often these elements are developed using similar tasks and scenarios involving quests, monsters, and loot.

Progression

In nearly all MMORPGs, the development of the player's character is a primary goal. Nearly all MMORPGs feature a character progression system in which players earn experience points for their actions and use those points to reach character "levels", which makes them better at whatever they do.[] Traditionally, combat with monsters and completing quests for NPCs, either alone or in groups, are the primary ways to earn experience points. The accumulation of wealth (including combat-useful items) is also a way to progress in many MMORPGs, and again, this is traditionally best accomplished via combat. The cycle produced by these conditions, combat leading to new items allowing for more combat with no change in gameplay, is sometimes pejoratively referred to as the level treadmill, or "grinding". The role-playing game *Progress Quest* was created as a parody of this trend. *Eve Online* trains skills in real time rather than using experience points as a meter of progression.

In some MMORPGs, there is no limit to a player's level, allowing the grinding experience to continue indefinitely. MMORPGs that use this model often glorify top ranked players by displaying their avatars on the game's website or posting their stats on a high score screen. Another common practice is to enforce a maximum reachable level for all players, often referred to as a cap. Once reached, the definition of a player's progression changes. Instead of being awarded primarily with experience for completing quests and dungeons, collecting money and equipment will replace the player's motivation to continue playing.

Often, the widened range of equipment available at the maximum level will have increased aesthetic value to distinguish high ranking players in game. Colloquially known as endgame gear, this set of empowered weapons and armor adds a competitive edge to both scripted boss encounters as well as player vs. player combat. Player motivation to outperform others is fueled by acquiring such items and is a significant determining factor in their success or failure in combat related situations.

Also, traditional in the genre is the eventual demand on players to team up with others in order to progress at the optimal rate. This sometimes forces players to change their real-world schedules in order to "keep up" within the game-world. A good example of this is the need to trade items to achieve certain goals, or teaming up to kill a powerful enemy.

Social Interaction

MMORPGs almost always have tools to facilitate communication between players. Many MMORPGs offer support for in-game guilds or clans (though these will usually form whether the game supports them or not).

In addition, most MMOs require some degree of teamwork for parts of the game. These tasks usually require players to take on roles in the group, such as those protecting other players from damage (called tanking), "healing" damage done to other players or damaging enemies.

MMORPGs generally have Game Moderators or Game Masters (frequently abbreviated to GM), who may be paid employees or unpaid volunteers who attempt to supervise the world. Some GMs may have additional access to features and information related to the game that are not available to other players and roles.

Roleplaying

Most MMORPGs provide different types of classes that players can choose. Among those classes, a small portion of players choose to roleplay their characters, and there are rules that provide functionality and content to this end. Community resources such as forums and guides exist in support of this play style.

For example, if a player wants to play a priest role in his MMORPG world, he might buy a cope from a shop and learn priestly skills, proceeding to speak, act, and interact with others as their character would. This may or may not include pursuing other goals such as wealth or experience. Guilds or similar groups with a focus on roleplaying may develop extended in-depth narratives using the setting and resources of the game world.

Culture

Over time, the MMORPG community has developed a sub-culture with its own slang and metaphor, as well as an unwritten list of social rules and taboos. Players will often complain about 'grind' (a slang term for any repetitive, time-consuming activity in an MMORPG), or talk about 'buffs' and 'nerfs' (respectively an upgrade or downgrade of a particular game mechanic). Social rules exist for such things as invitations to join an adventuring party, the proper division of treasure, and how a player is expected to behave while grouped with other players.

Debate rages in various gaming media over the long-term impact of MMORPG addiction; though reports exist of players that have neglected social, employment and/or family responsibilities in favor of their 'virtual lives', most have been debunked as 'urban legend', or at the very least highly embellished.

System architecture

Most MMORPGs are deployed using a client–server system architecture. The server software generates a persistent instance of the virtual world that runs continuously, and players connect to it via client software. The client software may provide access to the entire playing world, or further 'expansions' may be required to be purchased to allow access to certain areas of the game. *EverQuest* and *Guild Wars* are two examples of games that use such a format. Players generally must purchase the client software for a one-time fee, although an increasing trend is for MMORPGs to work using pre-existing "thin" clients, such as a web browser.

Some MMORPGs require payment of a monthly subscription to play. By nature, "massively multiplayer" games are always online, and most require some sort of continuous revenue (such as monthly subscriptions and advertisements) for maintenance and development. Some games, such as *Guild Wars* have disposed of the 'monthly fee' model entirely, and recover costs directly through sales of the software and associated expansion packs. Still others adopt a micropayment model where the core content is free, but players are given the option to purchase additional content, such as equipment, aesthetic items, or pets. Games that make use of this model often have originated in Korea, such as *Flyff* and *MapleStory*. This business model is alternately called "pay for perks" or "freemium", and games using it often describe themselves with the term "free-to-play".

Depending on the number of players and the system architecture, an MMORPG might actually be run on multiple separate servers, each representing an independent world, where players from one server cannot interact with those from another; *World of Warcraft* is a prominent example, with each separate server housing several thousand players. In many MMORPGs the number of players in one world is often limited to around a few thousand, but a notable example of the opposite is *EVE Online* which accommodates several hundred thousand players on the same server, with over 60,000 playing simultaneously (June 2010[5]) at certain times. Some games allow characters to appear on any world, but not simultaneously (such as *Seal Online: Evolution*), others limit each character to the world in which it was created. *World of Warcraft* has experimented with "cross-realm" (i.e. cross-server) interaction in PvP "battlegrounds", using server clusters or "battlegroups" to co-ordinate players looking to participate in structured PvP content such as the Warsong Gulch or Alterac Valley battlegrounds.[6] Additionally, patch 3.3, released on December 8, 2009, introduced a cross-realm "looking for group" system to help players form groups for instanced content (though not for open-world questing) from a larger pool of characters than their home server can necessarily provide.[7]

History

The term MMORPG was coined by Richard Garriott, the creator of *Ultima Online*, in 1997.[8] Previous to this and related coinages, these games were generally called graphical MUDs; the history of MMORPGs traces back directly through the MUD genre.[9] [10] Through this connection, MMORPGs can be seen to have roots in the earliest multi-user games such as Mazewar (1974) and *MUD1* (1978). 1985 saw the release of a roguelike (pseudo-graphical) MUD called *Island of Kesmai* on CompuServe[] and Lucasfilm's graphical MUD Habitat. The first fully graphical multi-user RPG was *Neverwinter Nights*, which was delivered through America Online in 1991

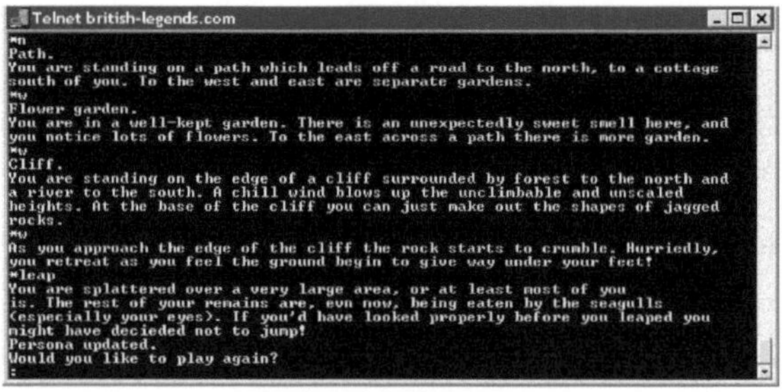

MUD1, an early multi-user game

and was personally championed by AOL President Steve Case.[] Other early proprietary graphical online RPGs include three on The Sierra Network: *The Shadow of Yserbius* in 1992, *The Fates of Twinion* in 1993, and *The Ruins of Cawdor* in 1995. Another milestone came in 1995 as NSFNET restrictions were lifted, opening the Internet up for game developers, which allowed for the first truly "massively"-scoped titles. Finally, MMORPGs as defined today began with *Meridian 59* in 1996, innovative both in its scope and in offering first-person 3D graphics, with *The Realm Online* appearing nearly simultaneously.[] *Ultima Online*, released in 1997, is often credited with first popularizing the genre,[] though more mainstream attention was garnered by 1999's *EverQuest* and *Asheron's Call* in the West[] and 1996's *Nexus: The Kingdom of the Winds* in South Korea.

These early titles' financial success has ensured competition in the genre since that time. MMORPG titles now exist on consoles and in new settings, and their players enjoy higher-quality gameplay. The current market for MMORPGs has Blizzard Entertainment's *World of Warcraft* dominating as the largest MMORPG,[11] alongside earlier such titles like *Final Fantasy XI* and *Guild Wars 2*, though an additional market exists for free-to-play MMORPGs, which are supported by advertising and purchases of in-game items. This free-to-play model is particularly common in South Korean MMORPGs such as *MapleStory*, *Rohan: Blood Feud*, and *Atlantica Online*. Also, there are some free-to-play games, such as *RuneScape* & *Tibia*, where the game is free, but one would have to pay monthly to play the game with more features. *Guild Wars* is an exception. It avoids some degree of competition with other MMORPGs by only requiring the initial purchase of the game to play.

Psychology

Since the interactions between MMORPG players are real, even if the environments are virtual, psychologists and sociologists are able to use MMORPGs as tools for academic research. Sherry Turkle, a clinical psychologist, has conducted interviews with computer users including game-players. Turkle found that many people have expanded their emotional range by exploring the many different roles (including gender identities) that MMORPGs allow a person to explore.[]

Nick Yee has surveyed more than 35,000 MMORPG players over the past several years, focusing on psychological and sociological aspects of these games. Recent findings included that 15% of players become a guild-leader at one time or another, but most generally find the job tough and thankless;[] and that players spend a considerable amount of time (often a third of their total time investment) doing things that are external to gameplay but part of the metagame.[]

Many players report that the emotions they feel while playing an MMORPG are very strong, to the extent that 8.7% of male and 23.2% of female players in a statistical study have had an online wedding.[12] Other researchers have found that the enjoyment of a game is directly related to the social organization of a game, ranging from brief encounters between players to highly organized play in structured groups.[13]

In a study by Zaheer Hussain and Mark D. Griffiths, it was found that just over one in five gamers (21%) said they preferred socializing online to offline. Significantly more male gamers than female gamers said that they found it easier to converse online than offline. It was also found that 57% of gamers had created a character of the opposite gender, and it is suggested that the online female persona has a number of positive social attributes.[14]

Richard Bartle, author of *Designing Virtual Worlds*, classified multiplayer RPG-players into four primary psychological groups. His classifications were then expanded upon by Erwin Andreasen, who developed the concept into the thirty-question Bartle Test that helps players determine which category they are associated with. With over 650,000 test responses as of 2011, this is perhaps the largest ongoing survey of multiplayer game players.[] Based on Bartle and Yee's research, Jon Radoff has published an updated model of player motivation that focuses on immersion, competition, cooperation and achievement.[15] [16] These elements may be found not only in MMORPGs, but many other types of games and within the emerging field of gamification.

In *World of Warcraft*, a temporary design glitch attracted the attention of psychologists and epidemiologists across North America, when the "Corrupted Blood" disease of a monster began to spread unintentionally—and uncontrollably—into the wider game world. The Centers for Disease Control used the incident as a research model to chart both the progression of a disease, and the potential human response to large-scale epidemic infection.[]

Economics

Many MMORPGs feature living economies. Virtual items and currency have to be gained through play and have definite value for players.[] Such a virtual economy can be analyzed (using data logged by the game)[] and has value in economic research; more significantly, these "virtual" economies can have an impact on the economies of the real world.

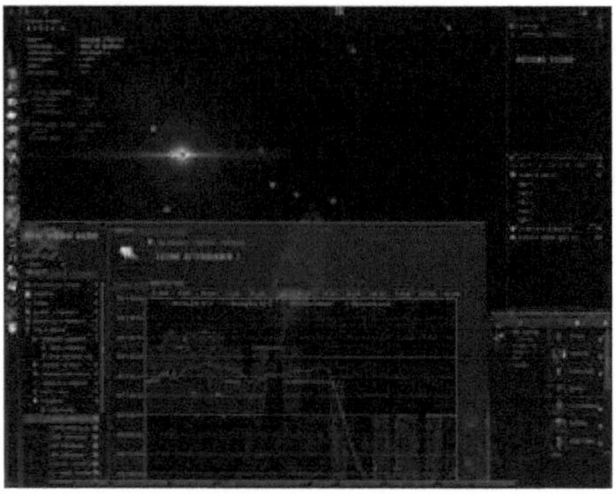

A user browsing the market for items in EVE Online

One of the early researchers of MMORPGs was Edward Castronova, who demonstrated that a supply-and-demand market exists for virtual items and that it crosses over with the real world.[17] This crossover has some requirements of the game:

- The ability for players to sell an item to each other for in-game (virtual) currency.
- Bartering for items between players for items of similar value.
- The purchase of in-game items for real-world currency.
- Exchanges of real-world currencies for virtual currencies.
- The invention of user-created meta-currencies such as Dragon kill points to distribute in-game rewards.[18]

The idea of attaching real-world value to "virtual" items has had a profound effect on players and the game industry, and even the courts.[19] The Virtual currency selling pioneer IGE received a lawsuit from a World of Warcraft player for interfering in the economics and intended use of the game by selling wow gold.[] Castronova's first study in 2002 found that a highly liquid (if illegal) currency market existed, with the value of *Everquest*'s in-game currency exceeding that of the Japanese yen.[] Some people even make a living by working these virtual economies; these people are often referred to as gold farmers, and may be employed in game sweatshops.[]

Game publishers usually prohibit the exchange of real-world money for virtual goods, but others actively promote the idea of linking (and directly profiting from) an exchange. In *Second Life* and *Entropia Universe*, the virtual economy and the real-world economy are directly linked. This means that real money can be deposited for game money and vice versa. Real-world items have also been sold for game money in *Entropia*, and some players of *Second Life* have generated revenues in excess of $100,000.[]

Some of the issues confronting online economies include:

- The use of "bots" or automated programs, that assist some players in accumulating in-game wealth to the disadvantage of other players.[20]
- The use of unsanctioned auction sites, which has led publishers to seek legal remedies to prevent their use based on intellectual-property claims.[21]
- The emergence of virtual crime, which can take the form of both fraud against the player or publisher of an online game, and even real-life acts of violence stemming from in-game transactions.[22]

Linking real-world and virtual economies is rare in MMORPGs, as it is generally believed to be detrimental to gameplay. If real-world wealth can be used to obtain greater, more immediate rewards than skillful gameplay, the incentive for strategic roleplay and real game involvement is diminished. It could also easily lead to a skewed hierarchy where richer players gain better items, allowing them to take on stronger opponents and level up more quickly than less wealthy but more committed players.[23]

Development

The cost of developing a competitive commercial MMORPG title often exceeded $10 million by 2003.[24] These projects require multiple disciplines within game design and development such as 3D modeling, 2D art, animation, user interfaces, client/server engineering, database architecture, and network infrastructure.[25]

Players interacting in *Ultima Online*, a classic MMORPG.

The front-end (or client) component of a commercial, modern MMORPG features 3D graphics. As with other modern 3D games, the front-end requires expertise with implementing 3D engines, real-time shader techniques and physics simulation. The actual visual content (areas, creatures, characters, weapons, spaceships and so forth) is developed by artists who typically begin with two-dimensional concept art, and later convert these concepts into animated 3D scenes, models and texture maps.[26]

Developing an MMOG server requires expertise with client/server architecture, network protocols, security, and database design. MMORPGs include reliable systems for a number of vital tasks. The server must be able to handle and verify a large number of connections, prevent cheating, and apply changes (bug fixes or added content) to the game. A system for recording the game's data at regular intervals, without stopping the game, is also important.[27]

Maintenance requires sufficient servers and bandwidth, and a dedicated support staff. Insufficient resources for maintenance lead to lag and frustration for the players, and can severely damage the reputation of a game, especially at launch. Care must also be taken to ensure that player population remains at an acceptable level by adding or removing servers. Peer-to-peer MMORPGs could theoretically work cheaply and efficiently in regulating server load, but practical issues such as asymmetrical network bandwidth, CPU-hungry rendering engines, unreliability of individual nodes, and inherent lack of security (opening fertile new grounds for cheating) make them a difficult proposition. The hosted infrastructure for a commercial-grade MMORPG requires the deployment of hundreds (or even thousands) of servers. Developing an affordable infrastructure for an online game requires developers to scale to large numbers of players with less hardware and network investment.[28]

In addition, the development team will need to have expertise with the fundamentals of game design: world-building, lore and game mechanics,[29] as well as what makes games fun.[30]

Non-corporate development

Though the vast majority of MMORPGs are produced by companies, many small teams of programmers and artists have contributed to the genre. As shown above, the average MMORPG development project requires enormous investments of time and money, and running the game can be a long-term commitment. As a result, non-corporate (or independent, or "indie") development of MMORPGs is less common compared with other genres. Still, many independent MMORPGs do exist, representing a wide spectrum of genres, gameplay types, and revenue systems.

Some independent MMORPG projects are completely open source, while others feature proprietary content made with an open-source game engine. The WorldForge project has been active since 1998 and formed a community of independent developers who are working on creating framework for a number of open-source MMORPGs.[31] The Multiverse Network is also creating a network and platform specifically for independent MMOG developers.[32]

Trends

As there are a number of wildly different titles within the genre, and since the genre develops so rapidly, it is difficult to definitively state that the genre is heading in one direction or another. Still, there are a few obvious developments. One of these developments is the raid group quest, or "raid",[] which is an adventure designed for large groups of players (often twenty or more).

Instance dungeons

Instance dungeons, sometimes shortened to "instances", are game areas that are "copied" for individual players or groups, which keeps those in the instance separated from the rest of the game world. This reduces competition, while also reducing the amount of data that needs to be sent to and from the server, reducing lag. *The Realm Online* was the first MMORPG to begin to use a rudimentary form of this technique and *Anarchy Online* would develop it further, using instances as a key element of gameplay. Since then, instancing has become increasingly common. The "raids", as mentioned above, often involve instance dungeons. Examples of games which feature instances are *World of Warcraft*, *The Lord of the Rings Online*, *EverQuest II*, *Aion*, *Guild Wars*, *RuneScape', "Star Trek Online", and* DC Universe Online.

Player-created content

Increased amounts of "player-created content" may be another trend.[33]

Use of licenses

The use of intellectual property licensing, common in other video game genres, has also appeared in MMORPGs. 2007 saw the release of *The Lord of the Rings Online*, based on J. R. R. Tolkien's Middle-earth. Other licensed MMORPGs include *The Matrix Online*, based on the *Matrix* trilogy of films, *Warhammer Online: Age of Reckoning*, based on Games Workshop's table top game, *Star Wars Galaxies*, *Star Wars The Old Republic*, *Champions Online* and *Age of Conan*.

Additionally, several licenses from television have been optioned for MMORPGs, for example *Star Trek Online* and *Stargate Worlds* (which was canceled).

Console-based MMORPGs

The first console-based MMORPG was *Phantasy Star Online* for the Sega Dreamcast. The first console-based open-world MMORPG was *Final Fantasy XI* for the Sony PlayStation 2. *EverQuest Online Adventures*, also on the PlayStation 2, was the first console MMORPG in North America. Although console-based MMORPGs are considered more difficult to produce,[] the platform is gaining more attention.

Browser-based MMORPGs

With the popularization of Facebook and microtransactions has come a new wave of Flash and HTML5 based MMORPGs that use the free to play model. They require no download outside of a browser and usually have heavily integrated social media sharing features.

Smartphone-based MMORPGs

Smartphones with their GPS capabilities (amongst others) enable augmented reality games such as Ingress.

See also

- Chronology of MUDs
- Comparison of massively multiplayer online role-playing games
- List of free massively multiplayer online games
- List of massively multiplayer online role-playing games
- List of text-based MMORPGs
- Server emulator
- Virtual good
- Virtual currency
- Virtual economy
- Virtual world

References

[6] World of Warcraft Europe -> Info -> Basics -> Battlegroups (http://web.archive.org/web/20080405235302/http://www.wow-europe.com/en/info/basics/battlegroups.html)
[7] World of Warcraft Europe -> Patch Notes - Patch 4.0.1 - 4.0.3a (http://www.wow-europe.com/en/patchnotes/)
[13] Nardi, Harris (2006), Strangers and Friends: Collaborative Play in World of Warcraft, Proceedings of the 2006 20th anniversary conference on Computer supported cooperative work
[14] Hussain, Zaheer (2008), Gender Swapping and Socializing in Cyberspace: An Exploratory Study
[15] Radoff, Jon. "Game Player Motivations." May 2011. http://radoff.com/blog/2011/05/19/game-player-motivations/
[16] Radoff, Jon. April 2011. *Game On: Energize Your Business with Social Games.* ISBN 978-0-470-93626-9
[20] Robert Shapiro (2003), How online games teach us about economics, slate.com (http://www.slate.com/id/2078053/)
[21] Blizzard Goes to War, terranova.blogs.com (http://terranova.blogs.com/terra_nova/2004/12/blizzard_goes_t.html)
[22] BBC News (2005), Game Theft led to Fatal Attack, news.bbc.co.uk (http://news.bbc.co.uk/2/hi/technology/4397159.stm)
[24] Adam Carpenter (2003), Applying Risk-Based Analysis to Play Balance RPGs, Gamasutra, gamasutra.com (http://www.gamasutra.com/view/feature/2843/applying_risk_analysis_to_.php)
[25] Jon Radoff (2007), "Anatomy of an MMORPG," *PlayerVox,* radoff.com (http://radoff.com/blog/2008/08/22/anatomy-of-an-mmorpg/)
[26] Frank Luna (2006), "3D Game Programming with DirectX 9.0c, a Shader Approach," Worldware Publishing, ISBN 1-59822-016-0
[27] Jay Lee (2003), Gamasutra, Relational Database Guidelines for MMOGs, gamasutra.com (http://www.gamasutra.com/resource_guide/20030916/lee_01.shtml)
[28] GDC Proceedings 2005, Online Game Architecture: Back-End Strategies, gamasutra.com (http://www.gamasutra.com/gdc2005/features/20050310/esbensen_01.shtml)
[29] Chris Crawford (2003), Chris Crawford on Game Design, New Riders Games, ISBN 0-13-146099-4
[33] Jon Radoff (March 20, 2007), Gamasutra, Five Prescriptions for Viral Games, gamasutra.com (http://www.gamasutra.com/view/feature/1693/five_prescriptions_for_viral_games.php)

External links

- The Daedalus Project (http://www.nickyee.com/daedalus) – Nick Yee's ongoing survey study of MMORPG players. Demographics, narratives and essays.
- Massively multiplayer online role-playing game (http://www.dmoz.org/Games/Video_Games/Roleplaying/Massive_Multiplayer_Online/) at the Open Directory Project

EverQuest

EverQuest	
Developer(s)	Sony Online Entertainment
Publisher(s)	Sony Online Entertainment
Platform(s)	Windows, Mac OS X (partial)
Release date(s)	16 March 1999
Genre(s)	Massively multiplayer online role-playing game
Mode(s)	Multiplayer online
Distribution	CD-ROM, DVD-ROM, download

EverQuest is a 3D fantasy-themed massively multiplayer online role-playing game (MMORPG) that was released on March 16, 1999. The original design is credited to Brad McQuaid, Steve Clover, and Bill Trost. It was developed by Sony's 989 Studios and its early-1999 spin-off Verant Interactive, and published by Sony Online Entertainment (SOE).[]

Since its acquisition of Verant in late 1999, SOE develops, runs, and distributes *EverQuest*.[] *EverQuest*'s development is ongoing, and the nineteenth expansion, *Rain of Fear*, launched November 28, 2012. Additional subscription options of *EverQuest*, free-to-play Bronze Level, and a one-time fee Silver Level, were made available in March 2012.[]

EverQuest has earned numerous awards, including 1999 GameSpot Game of the Year and a 2007 Technology & Engineering Emmy Award.[1]

Gameplay

Many of the elements in *EverQuest* have been drawn from text-based MUD (Multi-User Dungeon) games,[] particularly DikuMUDs, which in turn were inspired by traditional role-playing games such as *Dungeons & Dragons*. In *EverQuest*, players create a character (also known as an avatar, or colloquially as a *char* or *toon*) by selecting one of sixteen races in the game, which range from humans (basic human, Erudite, and barbarian), elves (high elves, wood elves, and dark elves), half-elves, dwarves, gnomes, halflings, trolls, and ogres of fantasy, to cat-people (Vah Shir), lizard-people (Iksar), frog-people (Froglok), and dragon-people (Drakkin).[] At creation, players select each character's adventuring occupation (such as a wizard, ranger, or cleric – called a *class* — see below for particulars), a patron deity, and starting city. Customization of the character facial appearance is available at creation (hair, hair color, face style, facial hair, facial hair color, eye color, etc.).

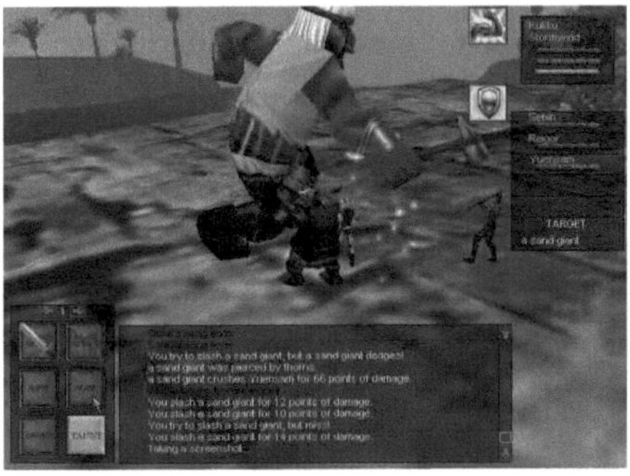

A Sand Giant engaging a group in the Oasis of Marr, a desert zone

Players use their character to explore the fantasy world of Norrath, fight monsters and enemies for treasure and experience points, and master trade skills. As they progress, players advance in level, gaining power, prestige, spells, and abilities through actions such as defeating capable opponents, looting the remains of defeated enemies and completing quests (tasks and adventures given by non-player characters (NPCs).

EverQuest allows players to interact with other people through role-play, joining player guilds, and dueling other players (in restricted situations – *EverQuest* only allows player versus player (PVP) combat on the PvP-specific server, specified arena zones and through agreed upon dueling).

The game-world of *EverQuest* consists of nearly four hundred zones.[2]

Multiple instances of the world exist on various servers. In the past, game server populations were visible during log-in, and showed peaks of more than 3000 players per server. The design of *EverQuest*, like other massively multiplayer online role-playing games, makes it highly amenable to cooperative play, with each player having a specific role within a given group.

Classes

The fourteen classes of the original 1999 version of *EverQuest* were later expanded to include the Beastlord and Berserker classes with the *Shadows of Luclin* (2001) and *Gates of Discord* (2004) expansions, respectively. The classes can be categorized based on similar characteristics that allow them to play certain types of roles within the game when grouped with others.

There are four classes which categorize as **tanks**. Members of this group have a high number of hitpoints for their level, and may wear heavy armor. The tank, or melee, classes include: Beserker, Shadowknight, Paladin, and Warrior. They have the ability to taunt enemies into focusing on them, rather than other party members who may be more susceptible to damage and death.

The **damage-dealing** classes are able to deal high corporeal damage to opponents. Within the game, these caster classes are often referred to as 'DPS', which stands for damage per second. There isn't a definitive 'best DPS' class, as damage dealt will depend on numerous factors which vary from one encounter to another (such as the enemy's armor, its positioning, and its magic resistance).

Caster classes have the lowest hit points per level and can only wear the lightest of armors. The four caster classes include: Enchanter, Magician, Necromancer, and Wizard. The casters draw their power from an internal pool of *mana*, which takes some time to regenerate and thus demands judicious and efficient use of spells. All caster classes have the ability to 'Research', an activity where all players can make spells for use by other players. These are made using assortments of different pieces of quest material found in the game.

Hybrid classes are able to use a wide variety of skills to support the other classes. Five classes fall into this category: Bard, Beastlord, Paladin, Ranger, and Shadowknight. All of these classes have the ability to melee as well as buff and heal. They make good solo or group characters. They can use a wide range of weapon types.

Priest, or **healer,** classes have medium level of hit points per level and have access to healing and buff spells. This category has three classes: Cleric, Druid, and Shaman.

Deities

There are several deities in *EverQuest* who each have a certain area of responsibility and play a role in the backstory of the game setting. A wide array of armor and weapons are also deity-tied, making it possible for only those who worship that deity to wear/equip them. Additionally, deities determine, to some extent, where characters may and may not go without being attacked on sight.

Zones

The *EverQuest* universe is divided into more than 375 zones.[] These zones represent a wide variety of geographical features, including plains, oceans, cities, deserts, and other planes of existence. One of the most popular zones in the game is the Plane of Knowledge, one of the few zones in which all races and classes can coexist harmoniously without interference. The Plane of Knowledge is also home to portals to many other zones, including portals to other planes and to the outskirts of nearly every starting city.

Development

EverQuest began as a concept by John Smedley in 1996.

EverQuest II was released in late 2004.[] Set in an alternate universe similar to that of the original EverQuest, this sequel takes place 500 years after the awakening of The Sleeper. The game has also inspired a number of other spin-offs.

The third iteration in the series, with the working title *EverQuest Next*, is currently in the early stages of development as first reported in the 2009 *10th Anniversary EverQuest Book*.[3] At the SOE Fan Faire in August 2010, in-game screenshots, concept art and more information was revealed.[4] However, since then it's been revealed that this early version of the game was scrapped and a new design is being implemented. More details are expected at SOE Live, which is scheduled for August 1–4, 2013.

History

The design and concept of *EverQuest* is heavily indebted to text-based MUDs, in particular DikuMUD, and as such *EverQuest* is considered a 3D evolution of the text MUD genre like some of the MMOs that preceded it, such as *Meridian 59* and *The Realm Online*. John Smedley, Brad McQuaid, Steve Clover and Bill Trost, who jointly are credited with creating the world of *EverQuest*, have repeatedly pointed to their shared experiences playing MUDs such as *Sojourn* and *TorilMUD* as the inspiration for the game.[] Keith Parkinson created the box covers for earlier installments of EverQuest.

Development of *EverQuest* began in 1996 when Sony Interactive Studios America (SISA) executive John Smedley secured funding for a 3D game like text-based MUDs following the successful launch of *Meridian 59* the previous year. To implement the design, Smedley hired programmers Brad McQuaid and Steve Clover, who had come to Smedley's attention through their work on the single player RPG *Warwizard*. McQuaid soon rose through the ranks to become executive producer for the *EverQuest* franchise and emerged during development of *EverQuest* as a popular figure among the fan community through his in-game avatar, Aradune. Other key members of the development team included Bill Trost, who created the history, lore and major characters of Norrath (including *EverQuest* protagonist Firiona Vie), Geoffrey "GZ" Zatkin, who implemented the spell system, and artist Milo D. Cooper, who did the original character modeling in the game.

EverQuest launched with modest expectations from Sony on 16 March 1999 under its Verant Interactive brand and quickly became successful. By the end of the year, it had surpassed competitor *Ultima Online* in number of subscriptions. Numbers continued rising rapidly until mid-2001 when growth slowed. Sony's last reported subscription numbers were given as more than 430,000 players on 14 January 2004.[5] SOE released a Mac OS X version of *EverQuest* in 2003, incorporating all expansions through Planes of Power.

EverQuest initially launched with volunteer "Guides" who would act as basic customer service/support via 'petitions'. Issues could be forwarded to the Game Master assigned to the server or resolved by the volunteer. Other guides would serve in administrative functions within the program or assisting the Quest Troupe with dynamic and persistent live events throughout the individual servers. Volunteers were compensated with free subscription and expansions to the game. In 2003 the program changed for the volunteer guides taking them away from the customer service focus and placing them into their current roles as roving 'persistant characters' role-playing with the players.

In anticipation of PlayStation's launch, Sony Interactive Studios America made the decision to focus primarily on console titles under the banner 989 Studios, while spinning off its sole computer title, *EverQuest*, which was ready to launch, to a new computer game division named Redeye (renamed Verant Interactive). Executives initially had very low expectations for *EverQuest*, but in 2000, following the surprising continued success and unparalleled profits of *EverQuest*, Sony reorganized Verant Interactive into Sony Online Entertainment (SOE) with Smedley retaining control of the company.

Many of the original *EverQuest* team, including Brad McQuaid, Steve Clover and Geoffrey Zatkin left SOE by 2002.

Subscriptions

Verant, from 1999 to 2001, and SOE, from 2001 to 14 January 2004, issued formal statements giving some indications of the number of *EverQuest* subscriptions and peak numbers of players online at any given moment.[5] These records show more than 225,000 subscriptions on 1 November 1999, with an increase to more than 450,000 subscriptions by 25 September 2003.

On June 6, 2012, SOE removed the ability to buy game subscription time with Station Cash without any warning to players. SOE apologized for this abrupt change in policy and reinstated the option for an additional week, after which it was removed permanently.[6]

Expansions

There have been 19 expansions to the original game since release. Expansions are purchased separately and provide additional content to the game (for example: raising the maximum character level; adding new races, classes, zones, continents, quests, equipment, game features). Additionally, the game is updated through downloaded patches. The *EverQuest* expansions:

1. *The Ruins of Kunark* (April 2000)
2. *The Scars of Velious* (December 2000)
3. *The Shadows of Luclin* (December 2001)
4. *The Planes of Power* (October 2002)
5. *The Legacy of Ykesha* (February 2003)
6. *Lost Dungeons of Norrath* (September 2003)
7. *Gates of Discord* (February 2004)
8. *Omens of War* (September 2004)
9. *Dragons of Norrath* (February 2005)
10. *Depths of Darkhollow* (September 2005)
11. *Prophecy of Ro* (February 2006)
12. *The Serpent's Spine* (September 2006)
13. *The Buried Sea* (February 2007)
14. *Secrets of Faydwer* (November 2007)
15. *Seeds of Destruction* (October 2008)
16. *Underfoot* (December 2009)
17. *House of Thule* (October 2010)
18. *Veil of Alaris* (November 2011)

19. *Rain of Fear* (November 2012) and *Shadow of Fear* (April 2013) and *Heart of Fear* (July 2013)
20. Call of the Forsaken(September 2013)

Servers

The game runs on multiple game servers, each with a unique name for identification. These names were originally the deities of the world of Norrath. In technical terms, each game server is actually a cluster of server machines. Once a character is created, it can be played only on that server unless the character is transferred to a new server by the customer service staff, generally for a fee. Each server often has a unique community and people often include the server name when identifying their character outside of the game.

OS X

SOE devoted one server (Al'Kabor) to an OS X version of the game. In January 2012, SOE announced plans to shut down the server, but based on the passionate response of the player base, rescinded the decision and changed Al'Kabor to a free-to-play subscription model.[7] At about the same time, SOE revised the Macintosh client software to run natively on Intel processors. Players running on older, PowerPC-based systems lost access to the game at that point.[8]

For several years in the early existence of Al'Kabor, an "EverQuest for Macintosh" subscription did not allow the subscriber to create posts on the official Sony "EverQuest for Macintosh" forums.[9] Out-of-game discussions thus took root at another location that became an online source of information for technical issues, as well as for the various gameplay and sociological aspects that are unique to "EverQuest for Macintosh".[10]

European

Two SOE servers were set up to better support players in and around Europe: Antonius Bayle and Kane Bayle. Kane Bayle was merged into Antonius Bayle.

With the advent of the *New Dawn* promotion, three additional servers were set up and maintained by Ubisoft: Venril Sathir (British), Sebilis (French) and Kael Drakkal (German). The downside of the servers was that while it was possible to transfer to them, it was impossible to transfer off.

The servers were subsequently acquired by SOE and all three were merged into Antonius Bayle server.[11]

Controversies, social issues, and game problems

Sale of in-game objects/real world economics

EverQuest has been the subject of various criticisms. One example involves the sale of in-game objects for real currency (often through eBay). The developers of *EQ* have always forbidden the practice.

Because items can be traded within the game and also because of illegal online trading on websites, virtual currency to real currency exchange rates have been calculated. The BBC reported that in 2002 work done by Edward Castronova showed that *EverQuest* was the 77th richest country in the world, sandwiched between Russia and Bulgaria and its GDP per capita was higher than that of the People's Republic of China and India.[12] In 2004, a follow-up analysis of the entire online gaming industry indicated that the combined GDP of the online "worlds" populated by the two million players was approximately the same as that of Namibia.[13]

Companies created characters, leveled them to make them powerful, and then resold the characters or specialized in exchanging money between games. A player could exchange a house in *The Sims Online* for *EverQuest* platinum pieces, depending solely on market laws of supply and demand.

Sony officially discourages the payment of real-world money for online goods, except on certain "Station Exchange" servers in *EverQuest II*, launched in July 2005. The program facilitates buying in-game items for real money from fellow players for a nominal fee. At this point this system only applies to select *EverQuest II* servers; none of the pre-*Station Exchange EverQuest II* or *EverQuest* servers are affected.[14]

Intellectual property and role-playing

Another well-publicized incident from October 2000, usually referred to as the "Mystere incident", involved Verant banning a player for creating controversial fan fiction, causing outrage among *EverQuest* players and sparking a major industry-wide debate about players' rights and the line between roleplaying and intellectual property infringement. The case was used by several academics in discussing such rights in the digital age.[15]

Fans have created the open source server emulator EQEmu, allowing users to run their own servers with custom rules.

Addiction

The game is renowned and berated (by some psychologists specializing in computer addiction) for its addictive qualities. Many players refer to it half-jokingly as "EverCrack" (a disparaging comparison to crack cocaine).[16] There has been one well-publicized suicide of an *EverQuest* user named Shawn Woolley that resulted in his mother, Liz, founding Online Gamers Anonymous.[] []

Sociological aspects of MMORPGs

Massively multiplayer online role-playing games (MMORPGs) are described by some players[] as "chat rooms with a graphical interface". The sociological aspects of *EverQuest* (and other MMORPGs) are explored in a series of online studies on a site known as "the HUB".[] The studies make use of data gathered from player surveys and discuss topics like virtual relationships, player personalities, gender issues, and more.

Organized protests

In May 2004, Woody Hearn of GU Comics called for all *EverQuest* gamers to boycott the *Omens of War* expansion in an effort to force SOE to address existing issues with the game rather than release another "quick-fire" expansion.[17] The call to boycott was rescinded after SOE held a summit to address player concerns, improve (internal and external) communication, and correct specific issues within the game.

Prohibition in Brazil

On 17 January 2008, the Judge of the 17th Federal Court of Minas Gerais State forbade the sales of the game in the whole Brazilian territory. The reason was that the game leads the players to a loss of moral virtue and takes them into "heavy" psychological conflicts because of the game quests.[18]

EverQuest universe

Since *EverQuest*'s release, Sony Online Entertainment has added several *EverQuest*-related games. These include:

- *EverQuest Hero's Call* (Pocket PC, January 2003)
- *EverQuest Online Adventures* (PlayStation 2, February 2003)
- *Lords of EverQuest* (PC, December 2003)
- *Champions of Norrath* (PlayStation 2, February 2004)
- *EverQuest Hero's Call 2* (Pocket PC, April 2004)
- *EverQuest II* (PC, November 2004)
- *Champions: Return to Arms*, sequel to *Champions of Norrath* (PlayStation 2, February 2005)
- *EverQuest Role-Playing Game* (a role-playing game produced in collaboration with White Wolf which uses the d20 system).

- *Legends of Norrath* (a virtual card game which launched sometime in 2007 or early 2008 which also awards EverQuest and EverQuest II players with in-game items).
- *EverQuest Next* (newest announced EverQuest game.)

A line of novels have been published in the world of *EverQuest*, including:

- *Rogue's Hour*, by Scott Ciencin (October 2004)
- *Ocean of Tears*, by Stewart Wieck (October 2005)
- *Truth and Steel*, by Thomas M. Reid (September 2006)
- *The Blood Red Harp*, by Elaine Cunningham (October 2006)

Notes

[5] Champions Of Norrath Announcement, Sony.com (http://championsofnorrath.station.sony.com/headset.jsp)

[6] Non-recurring Subscriptions Removal (http://forums.station.sony.com/eq/posts/list.m?topic_id=187127) Official news and announcements - 2012-06-15

[7] EQMac will carry on! (http://forums.station.sony.com/eq/posts/list.m?topic_id=183277), SOE forums

[8] EQMac Login News (http://forums.station.sony.com/eq/posts/list.m?topic_id=186138), SOE forums

[10] See, EQ MAC Gets a New Community Manager (http://forums.station.sony.com/eq/posts/list.m?topic_id=183492), SOE forums

[15] cf. Garlick M., "Player, Pirate or Conducer? A consideration of the rights of online gamers", *Yale Journal of Law & Technology*, 2004-2005.

External links

- Official *EverQuest* news (https://www.everquest.com/news/)

Warhammer_Online:_Age_of_Reckoning

Warhammer Online: Age of Reckoning	
Developer(s)	Mythic Entertainment
Publisher(s)	Electronic Arts
Designer(s)	Mark Jacobs Paul Barnett Jeff Hickman
Series	*Warhammer Fantasy*
Engine	Gamebryo engine
Platform(s)	Microsoft Windows, Mac OS X
Release date(s)	**Microsoft Windows** September 18, 2008[1] **OS X** July 30, 2009 (Beta)[2]
Genre(s)	MMORPG
Mode(s)	Multiplayer
Distribution	DVD, direct download

Warhammer Online: Age of Reckoning (officially abbreviated as *WAR*[3]) is a massively multiplayer online role-playing game based on Games Workshop's *Warhammer Fantasy* setting. It was developed by Mythic Entertainment and was simultaneously released in North and South Americas, Europe, Asia, Australia and New Zealand on September 18, 2008.[1] The game revolves around the continual worldwide conflict that the Warhammer Fantasy setting is known for, and the game is geared toward ongoing, constant war laced with dark humour.

Another ***Warhammer Online*** game which has been titled as *Warhammer Online: Wrath of Heroes* is a free-to-play multiplayer online battle arena game. However, the game was shut down during beta on March 29, 2013. [4]

Gameplay

Warhammer Online: Age of Reckoning features Mythic's Realm versus Realm (RvR) combat system, originally developed in *Dark Age of Camelot*.[5] This takes place within three different racial pairings: Dwarfs vs. Greenskins, Empire vs. Chaos, and High Elves vs. Dark Elves. Although there are only two races per pairing, players may travel to either of the other two pairings to help fight with their friends and allies. There are four types of RvR combat: Skirmishes (random world encounters), Battlefields (objective-driven battles in RvR-specific areas), Scenarios (instanced, point-based battles against the opposing faction), and Campaigns (invading enemy lands and capital cities). RvR contribution includes both Player vs. Player (PvP) combat *and* (to a lesser extent) Player vs. Environment (PvE) quests so that you can assist your realm in their victory, regardless of preferred play-style.

All activities in *WAR* contribute to the campaign, as it is the primary focus of the game. Each of the aforementioned activities generate Victory Points (VP) which measure a realm's progress in capturing a zone. When one realm reaches a designated amount of Victory Points in a particular zone, that zone falls under their control and the war pushes deeper into enemy territory. This back and forth struggle for zone control continues until one side holds two racial pairings, and the attacking side may sack, loot, and pillage the enemy's capital city. The capture of a capital city is the pinnacle objective of the campaign. Once a capital city is taken, the attackers are given a period time to loot the city. When this period expires, the defeated players receive increasing support from NPC guards until they are able to force the attackers out of their city and close the gates. At this point the campaign then begins anew, restarting the cycle.

Mythic also prevents the ganking of new players by more experienced players. For example, in Scenarios, low-level players may be boosted to an average level of play to ensure a more level playing field. Also, if a higher-ranked player enters an RvR zone specifically designated for lower level characters, they will be penalized by being temporarily transformed into a chicken. The players within those areas (which could be lower or equal level to the transformed player) can then ignore the transformed player, or dispatch the chicken with one blow.

WAR features a "Tome of Knowledge" (ToK) that is an extension upon similar mechanisms in many other MMOs. The ToK is a multi-purpose reference tool that is designed to provide the player with a great deal of information about the game world. It is also meant to serve as a reduction in the need for players to feel like they have to rely upon third-party sources of information pertaining to the game.[6]

Armies

Warhammer Online: Age of Reckoning is a Realm versus Realm (RvR) game with two factions: Order and Destruction. Each faction contains three separate armies, each of which is further broken down into four career choices.[3]

Armies of Order

Dwarfs – The army of the Dwarfs in WAR is known as the Oathbearers, named because of their oath of allegiance to the High King. Their duty was to find necessary materials in the most dangerous places in the world, requiring exceptional Dwarves to undertake such a task.[7]

Empire – The Order of the Griffon is the Empire army involved in WAR, formed by Emperor Karl Franz with the blessing of the Church of Sigmar, the Colleges of Magic and the Reiksguard. The Order is primarily made up of knights, warrior priests of Sigmar and wizards charged with defending the realm, and are answerable only to the Emperor himself.[8]

High Elves – In WAR, high elf characters are part of an army known as the Shining Guard, under the command of the legendary warrior Prince Tyrion. They were tasked with defending Ulthuan while the Phoenix King and his army fights alongside the Empire.[9]

Armies of Destruction

Greenskins (Orcs and Goblins) – The Greenskins are part of the Bloody Sun Boyz, led by the Black Orc Grumlok and his Goblin Shaman Gazbag. Their war with their old enemies, the Dwarfs, was manipulated by the Witch King Malekith. His intention was to start a war between the Greenskins and Dwarfs so that the Dwarfs could not come to the aid of the Empire, who would be forced to call upon the armies of the Phoenix King for aid – thus leaving Ulthuan ripe for the taking.[10]

Chaos – All Chaos players are affiliated to Tzeentch, as that is the patron deity of the Chaos force in WAR – the Raven Host. These are Tzeentch's most devoted servants, and its leader Tchar'zanek is one of the Lord of Magic's Chosen. Mainly these humans come from Norsca.[11]

Dark Elves – All Dark Elf players in WAR are members of House Uthorin, one of the noble families of Naggaroth. Their leader, Lord Uthorin, is a master of intrigue and has his sights set on Malekith's throne. But the Witch King has plans of his own.[12]

Skaven

A new "expansion" type feature released in 2010 lets you play in a skaven skin during tier 4 oRvR.

Careers

Each of the careers (classes) in *Warhammer Online* conform to an archetype role. For example, the Warrior Priest is an archetypal support or healer career, though he also has many melee DPS elements. In this way, the careers are given variety and avoid being simple reiterations of common archetypes.

There are specialization within careers, based on career mastery lines. This allows for more variation between characters of the same career.

Most careers have the option to play as either a male or female character. However, some careers such as the Witch Elf are only able to be played as one gender (female, in this case). By contrast, the Greenskins (Orcs and Goblins) are genderless, though masculine in appearance.

WAR Career Chart

Armies	Tank	Melee DPS	Ranged DPS	Healer/Support
Dwarfs	Ironbreaker [13]	Slayer (Male Only) [14]	Engineer [15]	Runepriest [16]
The Empire	Knight of the Blazing Sun [17]	Witch Hunter [18]	Bright Wizard [19]	Warrior Priest [20]
High Elves	Swordmaster [21]	White Lion [22]	Shadow Warrior [23]	Archmage [24]
Greenskins	Black Orc [25]	Choppa [26]	Goblin Squig Herder [27]	Goblin Shaman [28]
Chaos	Chosen (Male Only) [29]	Marauder (Male Only) [30]	Magus [31]	Zealot [32]
Dark Elves	Black Guard [33]	Witch Elf (Female Only) [34]	Sorceress/Sorcerer [35]	Disciple of Khaine [36]

Character customization

In *Warhammer Online* character customization is available in many forms. The initial character creation process allows players to select the race, career, and basic look of their character, including facial features and accessories. In addition to the original name that the player chooses for their character at creation, the player has the option to add a surname to their character for a small fee at rank 20. Dye is available at NPC vendors for recoloring **armor** and accessories. Players are able to decorate themselves with trophies, such as the heads of fallen enemies, which are equipped and displayed at various points on the character model.[37] Other forms of customization include Tactics (customizable sets of bonuses that players can adjust while out of combat), as well as Morale Abilities (increasingly powerful abilities that become available as morale is generated during the course of battle). Customizable armor and visual guild heraldry also aid in allowing a player to make their character visually unique.

In addition to visual character customization, Warhammer features an achievement system, similar to that of Steam. As achievements are unlocked, players may apply custom titles that appear beneath their names.

Collision detection

Warhammer Online features collision detection, a feature that is designed to prevent players from moving through other player characters. This feature works on enemy units as well as friendly units that are flagged for RvR combat. Collision detection enhances the role played by heavily armored characters known as "tanks", as it helps them become far more efficient at holding choke points and protecting weaker players in their group such as healers and casters.[38] To prevent griefing, collision detection is suppressed for players of the same realm who are not engaged in combat.

Servers

Mythic offered four different server types at launch: Core, Open RvR, Role-Play, and Open RvR/RP.[39] On *Core* servers, enemy factions can only attack each other if both players are flagged for RvR. Players are automatically flagged for RvR upon entering RvR-specific areas or enemy PvE areas, and can choose to turn their flag on at any time. *Open RvR* servers are flagged for RvR at all times, with few exceptions. *Role-Play* servers have the same rules as the *Core* servers, and players are encouraged to role-play their characters. Finally, *Open RvR/RP* servers follow the same rules as the *Open RvR* servers, and players are encouraged to role-play their characters.

Development

The second online game development began under the company Climax Online. The project was officially canceled in June 2004 when Games Workshop determined that the roll-out costs would be too high.[40] However, work on the game never actually stopped as Climax Online continued the project using their own funds until the company reported in late 2004 that the *Warhammer Online* project was shut down due to difficulty in securing a publishing agreement.

With the license available again, Games Workshop was approached by Mythic Entertainment, who were interested in acquiring the license and starting a new project from scratch. A long-standing relationship between several Games Workshop managers and the CEO of Mythic Mark Jacobs ensured that a deal was quickly reached. The *Warhammer Online* license was acquired by Mythic on May 18, 2005. Mythic would soon cancel its original follow-up project Imperator Online after gaining the Warhammer License.[41]

Warhammer Online: Age of Reckoning is not purely derived from either Warhammer Fantasy Battles or Warhammer Fantasy Roleplay or any other source alone, but rather from the Warhammer Fantasy universe as a whole.

Though *Warhammer Online: Age of Reckoning* is being developed by Mythic Entertainment, Games Workshop is also involved with the ongoing development of the project. Their role is not only to ensure that the project remains true to the *Warhammer Fantasy* IP, but also to work with Mythic to allow for the appropriate development and extension of the IP as necessitated for the MMO. Mythic has previously created MMOs, including *Dark Age of Camelot*.[42]

On July 30, 2009, Mythic Entertainment announced that *Warhammer Online* was being ported to the Mac OS X platform in the fall of 2009, with a beta version becoming available immediately. Like other Electronic Arts Mac games, *Warhammer Online* for Mac utilizes Cider technology by TransGaming Technologies.[2]

Community

Mythic has an official subscriber newsletter detailing the ongoing development of the game.[43]

The official website features a list of dedicated fansites [44] which allow them to interact with the community in addition to their own official forums [45]. The unofficial online community includes blogs, webcomics, forum/message boards, chat channels, wikis, and information databases.

During the development of *Warhammer Online*, Mythic featured a video blog of Creative Director Paul Barnett.[46] These videos gave the viewer an insight into the work that went on behind the scenes of *WAR*, often showcasing development screens and concept art for the game. Mythic also released "Development Diaries" from time to time, meant to give readers a deeper look into the ongoing development of *WAR*.[47]

Critical reception

Warhammer Online initially received favorable reviews. GameSpy gave it 5 out of 5 stars and claimed, "[it] has hit the ground running with one of the best MMO experiences we've had in a long time."[53] GameSpot gave it a 8.5 out of 10 and said, "Questers and explorers may not find what they're looking for, and certain gameplay systems don't mesh as well as they should. Nevertheless, there's more than enough exciting PvP content here to keep newcomers and veterans alike immersed in the perpetually violent tug of war between the forces of Order and Destruction."[52] Warhammer Online has an aggregate score of 86% on metacritic.com[49] and 87% GameRankings.com.[48]

As of September 30, 2008, *WAR* had sold 1.2 million copies and had 800,000 registered users.[55]

As of October 10, 2008, Mythic Entertainment announced that 750,000 people were playing Warhammer Online.[56]

As of December 31, 2008, the number of active *WAR* subscribers had decreased to "over 300,000 paying subscribers in North America and Europe."[57]

As of May 5, 2009, Electronic Arts executives confirmed in an investor conference that they have 300,000 subscribers as of the end of March 2009,[58] shortly after the company reported a loss of $1.08 billion in the financial year for 2009.[59] Consequently, the number of servers was drastically reduced[60] in order to consolidate the remaining population. The total number of servers was reduced to 13 and the number of role-playing servers was reduced to 1.[61]

Since this date, several servers were stopped, particularly in Europe, and there remained only 9 servers : 4 in the USA and 5 in Europe (including 2 in German & 1 in French).

As of February 9, 2011, 2 other U.S. Servers and 1 German server have been removed, leaving a total of 6 servers worldwide (2 in the US, 4 in Europe).[62]

Since December 14, 2011, the game is now down to 3 servers, one for the US, one for Germany and one for the rest of Europe.

Awards

Warhammer Online has received the following awards:[63]

2008

- IGN PC: Best of E3 2008-Best MMO
- IGN PC: 2008 Best Persistent World Game
- IGN PC: 2008 Reader's Choice
- Game Focus – Best MMO Game/ Expansion
- GameSpy: Best of E3 2008
- GameSpy: Best Use of License
- GameSpy: Top 10 PC Games – Ranked #2
- GameStooge – Best Massively Multiplayer Roleplaying Game
- G4TV: Best of E3 – PC
- Massively – Favorite New MMO of 2008
- MMORPG.com – Reader's Choice Awards – Best New Game of 2008
- MMORPG.com – Reader's Choice Awards – Most Innovative Feature
- MSNBC – Best PC games of 2008
- Voodoo Extreme: E3 2008 – Best MMO
- Warcry's Editor's Choice: Most Anticipated of 2008
- X-Play: Best MMO

2007

- Ten Ton Hammer: Best Fantasy MMOG
- Ten Ton Hammer: Best of Show
- Beckett Massive Online Game Reader's Choice Award: Most Anticipated MMO
- Warcry's Editor's Choice: 2007's Most Anticipated
- MMORPG.com Readers Choice: Most Anticipated

E3 2006

- MMORPG.com: Best Use Of A License
- Game Amp: Best of Show
- Game Amp: Best Loot
- Game Daily Nod Award
- Voodoo Extreme: Best Massively Multiplayer Game
- GameSpot Editor's Choice: Best Stage Demo
- Ten Ton Hammer Editor's Choice Award

References

[1] Mythic Entertainment (2008). Mythic announces Day of Reckoning (http://www.warhammeronline.com/pressreleases/20080805.php). Mythic Entertainment. Retrieved on 2008-08-06.
[2] Electronic Arts (2009). Apple Fans Prepare for War with Mac Version of Warhammer Online: Age of Reckoning (http://www.ea.com/news/mac-version-of-warhammer-online-age-of-reckoning). Electronic Arts. Retrieved on 2009-07-31.
[3] Mythic Entertainment (2007). Game Overview (http://www.warhammeronline.com/english/gameInfo/gameOverview/). Mythic Entertainment. Retrieved on 2007-02-01.
[5] GuildCafe (2007). Warhammer's Richard Duffek Talks about PvP and RvR (http://www.guildcafe.com/Vox/050507-Warhammer-Richard-Duffek-PVP-RVR.html). Retrieved on 2007-05-07.
[6] Mythic Entertainment (2008). Tome of Knowledge (http://www.warhammeronline.com/english/behindTheScenes/developmentDiaries/TomeofKnowledge.php). Mythic Entertainment. Retrieved on 2008-02-05.
[7] Mythic Entertainment (2007). The Dwarfs (http://www.warhammeronline.com/english/gameInfo/armiesofWAR/Dwarfs/Dwarfs.php). Mythic Entertainment. Retrieved on 2007-02-01.
[8] Mythic Entertainment (2007). The Empire (http://www.warhammeronline.com/english/gameInfo/armiesofWAR/Empire/Empire.php). Mythic Entertainment. Retrieved on 2007-02-01.
[9] Mythic Entertainment (2007). High Elves (http://www.warhammeronline.com/english/gameInfo/armiesofWAR/highelves/HighElf.php). Mythic Entertainment. Retrieved on 2008-04-02.
[10] Mythic Entertainment (2007). The Greenskins (http://www.warhammeronline.com/english/gameInfo/armiesofWAR/Greenskins/Greenskins.php). Mythic Entertainment. Retrieved on 2007-02-01.
[11] Mythic Entertainment (2007). Chaos (http://www.warhammeronline.com/english/gameInfo/armiesofWAR/Chaos/Chaos.php). Mythic Entertainment. Retrieved on 2007-02-01.
[12] Mythic Entertainment (2007). Dark Elves (http://www.warhammeronline.com/english/gameInfo/armiesofWAR/darkelves/DarkElf.php). Mythic Entertainment. Retrieved on 2008-04-02.
[13] http://www.warhammeronline.com/armiesofWAR/dwarfs/Ironbreaker.php
[14] http://www.warhammeronline.com/armiesofWAR/dwarfs/Slayer.php
[15] http://www.warhammeronline.com/armiesofWAR/dwarfs/DwarfEngineer.php
[16] http://www.warhammeronline.com/armiesofWAR/dwarfs/Runepriest.php
[17] http://www.warhammeronline.com/armiesofWAR/empire/KnightoftheBS.php
[18] http://www.warhammeronline.com/armiesofWAR/empire/WitchHunter.php
[19] http://www.warhammeronline.com/armiesofWAR/empire/BrightWizard.php
[20] http://www.warhammeronline.com/armiesofWAR/empire/warriorpriest.php
[21] http://www.warhammeronline.com/armiesofWAR/highelves/Swordmaster.php
[22] http://www.warhammeronline.com/armiesofWAR/highelves/WhiteLion.php
[23] http://www.warhammeronline.com/armiesofWAR/highelves/ShadowWarrior.php
[24] http://www.warhammeronline.com/armiesofWAR/highelves/Archmage.php
[25] http://www.warhammeronline.com/armiesofWAR/greenskins/BlackOrc.php
[26] http://www.warhammeronline.com/armiesofWAR/greenskins/OrcChoppa.php
[27] http://www.warhammeronline.com/armiesofWAR/greenskins/GoblinSquigHerder.php

[28] http://www.warhammeronline.com/armiesofWAR/greenskins/GoblinShaman.php
[29] http://www.warhammeronline.com/armiesofWAR/chaos/Chosen.php
[30] http://www.warhammeronline.com/armiesofWAR/chaos/Marauder.php
[31] http://www.warhammeronline.com/armiesofWAR/chaos/Magus.php
[32] http://www.warhammeronline.com/armiesofWAR/chaos/Zealot.php
[33] http://www.warhammeronline.com/armiesofWAR/darkelves/BlackGuard.php
[34] http://www.warhammeronline.com/armiesofWAR/darkelves/WitchElf.php
[35] http://www.warhammeronline.com/armiesofWAR/darkelves/Sorceress.php
[36] http://www.warhammeronline.com/armiesofWAR/darkelves/Disciple.php
[37] Mythic Entertainment(2008). The Trophy System (http://www.warhammeronline.com/english/behindTheScenes/developmentDiaries/Trophies.php). Mythic Entertainment. Retrieved on 2008-02-05.
[38] GameSpot (2007). Updated Hands-On: Bright Wizards, Magi, and More Player Versus Player" (http://www.gamespot.com/pc/rpg/warhammeronline/news.html?sid=6164998). GameSpot. Retrieved on 2007-02-01.
[39] Mythic Entertainment (2008). Server List and Rulesets (http://herald.warhammeronline.com/warherald/NewsArticle.war?id=252). Mythic Entertainment. Retrieved on 2009-02-24.
[40] GameSpot (2004). Warhammer Online Killed in Action (http://www.gamespot.com/pc/rpg/whonline/news.html?sid=6100992). GameSpot. Retrieved on 2007-02-01.
[41] Mythic Entertainment (2005). Mythic Entertainment Secures World Wide Rights to Create MMORPG Based on Games Workshop's Warhammer Fantasy World (http://www.warhammeronline.com/english/news/currentNews/05182005.php). Mythic Entertainment. Retrieved on 2007-02-01.
[42] Mythic Entertainment (2007). Mythic Entertainment Video Podcasts (http://www.warhammeronline.com/english/media/podcast/). Mythic Entertainment. Retrieved on 2007-12-27.
[43] Mythic Entertainment (2007). Newsletter Archives (http://www.warhammeronline.com/english/newsletterCentral/archives/). Mythic Entertainment. Retrieved on 2007-02-01.
[44] http://herald.warhammeronline.com/forumsfansites/index.php
[45] http://www.warhammeronline.com/forums/
[46] Mythic Entertainment(2007). Paul's Video Blog (http://www.warhammeronline.com/english/behindTheScenes/vidPhoneDiaries/index.php). Mythic Entertainment. Retrieved on 2007-02-01.
[47] Mythic Entertainment (2007). Development Diaries (http://www.warhammeronline.com/english/behindTheScenes/developmentDiaries/index.php). Mythic Entertainment. Retrieved on 2007-02-01.
[48] GameRankings.com (2008). Warhammer Online: Age of Reckoning Review (http://www.gamerankings.com/htmlpages2/520538.asp). Retrieved on 2008-10-04.
[49] Metacritic.com (2008). Warhammer Online: Age of Reckoning Review (http://www.metacritic.com/games/platforms/pc/warhammeronline). Retrieved on 2008-10-04.
[50] 1up.com (2008). Warhammer Online: Age of Reckoning Review (http://www.1up.com/do/reviewPage?cId=3170291). Retrieved on 2008-10-04.
[51] Eurogamer.com (2008). Warhammer Online: Age of Reckoning Review (http://www.eurogamer.net/article.php?article_id=234609). Retrieved on 2008-10-04.
[52] GameSpot.com (2008). Warhammer Online: Age of Reckoning Review (http://www.gamespot.com/pc/rpg/warhammeronline/index.html). Retrieved on 2008-10-04.
[53] GameSpy.com (2008). Warhammer Online: Age of Reckoning Review (http://pc.gamespy.com/pc/warhammer-online/914059p1.html). Retrieved on 2008-10-04.
[54] computerandvideogames.com (2008). Warhammer Online: Age of Reckoning Review (http://computerandvideogames.com/game.php?id=2909). Retrieved on 2008-10-04.
[56] AskMen.com (2008) (http://www.askmen.com/entertainment/gaming/pc/Warhammer-Online-Age-of-Reckoning/news-31-1.html)
[60] "Warhammer Online is 77% less online" (http://fidgit.com/archives/2009/03/warhammer-online-is-77-less-on.php)
[61] (http://herald.warhammeronline.com/warherald/NewsArticle.war?id=688)
[62] (http://herald.warhammeronline.com/warherald/NewsArticle.war?id=1490)
[63] Mythic Entertainment (2008). Awards (http://www.warhammeronline.com/awards/index.php). Mythic Entertainment. Retrieved on 2007-02-01.

namespace:The dot-com bubble in the United States

The **dot-com bubble** (also referred to as the **dot-com boom**, the **Internet bubble** and the **information technology bubble**[1]) was a historic speculative bubble covering roughly 1997–2000 (with a climax on March 10, 2000, with the NASDAQ peaking at 5408.60[2] in intraday trading before closing at 5048.62) during which stock markets in industrialized nations saw their equity value rise rapidly from growth in the Internet sector and related fields. While the latter part was a boom and bust cycle, the **Internet boom** is sometimes meant to refer to the steady commercial growth of the Internet with the advent of the World Wide Web, as exemplified by the first release of the Mosaic web browser in 1993, and continuing through the 1990s.

The period was marked by the founding (and, in many cases, spectacular failure) of a group of new Internet-based companies commonly referred to as *dot-coms*. Companies could cause their stock prices to increase by simply adding an "e-" prefix to their name or a ".com" to the end, which one author called "prefix investing".[3]

A combination of rapidly increasing stock prices, market confidence that the companies would turn future profits, individual speculation in stocks, and widely available venture capital created an environment in which many investors were willing to overlook traditional metrics such as P/E ratio in favor of confidence in technological advancements.

The collapse of the bubble took place during 2000–2001. Some companies, such as Pets.com, failed completely. Others lost a large portion of their market capitalization but remained stable and profitable, e.g., Cisco, whose stock declined by 86%. Some later recovered and surpassed their dot-com-bubble peaks, e.g., Amazon.com, whose stock went from 107 to 7 dollars per share, but a decade later exceeded 200.

Bubble growth

Venture capitalists saw record-setting growth as *dot-com* companies experienced meteoric rises in their stock prices and therefore moved faster and with less caution than usual, choosing to mitigate the risk by starting many contenders and letting the market decide which would succeed. The low interest rates in 1998–99 helped increase the start-up capital amounts. A canonical "dot-com" company's business model relied on harnessing network effects by operating at a sustained net loss and to build market share (or mind share). These companies offered their services or end product for free with the expectation that they could build enough brand awareness to charge profitable rates for their services later. The motto "get big fast" reflected this strategy.

Soaring stocks

In financial markets, a stock market bubble is a self-perpetuating rise or boom in the share prices of stocks of a particular industry. The term may be used with certainty only in retrospect when share prices have since crashed. A bubble occurs when speculators note the fast increase in value and decide to buy in anticipation of further rises, rather than because the shares are undervalued. Typically many companies thus become grossly overvalued. When the bubble "bursts", the share prices fall dramatically, and many companies go out of business.

American news media, including respected business publications such as *Forbes* and the *Wall Street Journal*, encouraged the public to invest in risky companies, despite many of the companies' disregard for basic financial and even legal principles.[4]

Andrew Smith argued that the financial industry's handling of IPOs tended to benefit the banks and initial investors rather than the company.[5] This is because company staff were typically barred from reselling their shares for a lock-in period of 12 to 18 months and so did not benefit from the common pattern of a huge short-lived spike in the share price on the day of the launch. By contrast, the financiers and other initial investors were typically entitled to sell at the peak price, and so could immediately profit from short-term price rises. Smith argues that the high profitability of the IPOs to Wall Street was a significant factor the course of events of the bubble. He writes:

> "But did the kids [the often young dotcom entrepreneurs] dupe the establishment by drawing them into fake companies, or did the establishment dupe the kids by introducing them to Mammon and charging a commission on it?"

In spite of this, however, a few company founders made vast fortunes when their companies were bought out at an early stage in the dot-com stock market bubble. These early successes made the bubble even more buoyant. An unprecedented amount of personal investing occurred during the boom, and the press reported the phenomenon of people quitting their jobs to become full-time day traders.[6] [7] [8]

Free spending

According to dot-com theory, an Internet company's survival depended on expanding its customer base as rapidly as possible, even if it produced large annual losses. For instance, Google and Amazon.com did not see any profit in their first years. Amazon was spending on expanding customer base and alerting people to its existence and Google was busy spending on creating more powerful machine capacity to serve its expanding search engine. The phrase "Get large or get lost" was the wisdom of the day.[9] At the height of the boom, it was possible for a promising dot-com to make an initial public offering (IPO) of its stock and raise a substantial amount of money even though it had never made a profit—or, in some cases, earned any revenue whatsoever. In such a situation, a company's lifespan was measured by its burn rate: that is, the rate at which a non-profitable company lacking a viable business model ran through its capital served as the metric.

Public awareness campaigns were one of the ways in which dot-coms sought to expand their customer bases. These included television ads, print ads, and targeting of professional sporting events. Many dot-coms named themselves with onomatopoeic nonsense words that they hoped would be memorable and not easily confused with a competitor. Super Bowl XXXIV in January 2000 featured 17 dot-com companies that each paid over $2 million for a 30-second spot. By contrast, in January 2001, just three dot-coms bought advertising spots during Super Bowl XXXV. In a similar vein, CBS-backed iWon.com gave away $10 million to a lucky contestant on an April 15, 2000 half-hour primetime special that was broadcast on CBS.

Not surprisingly, the "growth over profits" mentality and the aura of "new economy" invincibility led some companies to engage in lavish internal spending, such as elaborate business facilities and luxury vacations for employees. Executives and employees who were paid with stock options instead of cash became instant millionaires when the company made its initial public offering; many invested their new wealth into yet more dot-coms.

Cities all over the United States sought to become the "next Silicon Valley" by building network-enabled office space to attract Internet entrepreneurs. Communication providers, convinced that the future economy would require ubiquitous broadband access, went deeply into debt to improve their networks with high-speed equipment and fiber optic cables. Companies that produced network equipment like Nortel Networks were irrevocably damaged by such over-extension; Nortel declared bankruptcy in early 2009. Companies like Cisco, which did not have any production facilities, but bought from other manufacturers, were able to leave quickly and actually do well from the situation as the bubble burst and products were sold cheaply.

In the struggle to become a technology hub, many cities and states used tax money to fund technology conference centers, advanced infrastructure, and created favorable business and tax law to encourage development of the dotcom industry in their locale. Virginia's Dulles Technology Corridor is a prime example of this activity. Large quantities of high-speed fiber links were laid, and the State and local governments gave tax exemptions to technology firms. Many of these buildings could be viewed along I-495, after the burst, as vacant office buildings.

Similarly, in Europe the vast amounts of cash the mobile operators spent on 3G licences in Germany, Italy, and the United Kingdom, for example, led them into deep debt. The investments were far out of proportion to both their current and projected cash flow, but this was not publicly acknowledged until as late as 2001 and 2002. Due to the highly networked nature of the IT industry, this quickly led to problems for small companies dependent on contracts from operators. One example is of a then Finnish mobile network company Sonera, which paid huge sums in German broadband auction then dubbed as 3G licenses. Third-generation networks however took years to catch on and Sonera ended up as a part of TeliaSonera, then simply Telia.

The bubble bursts

Over 1999 and early 2000, the U.S. Federal Reserve increased interest rates six times,[10] and the economy began to lose speed. The dot-com bubble burst, numerically, on March 10, 2000, when the technology heavy NASDAQ Composite index, peaked at 5,048.62 (intra-day peak 5,408.60), more than double its value just a year before.[11] The NASDAQ fell slightly after that, but this was attributed to correction by most market analysts; the actual reversal and subsequent bear market may have been triggered by the adverse findings of fact in the *United States v. Microsoft* case which was being heard in federal court.[12] The conclusions of law, which declared Microsoft a monopoly, were widely expected in the weeks before their release on April 3.[13] The following day, April 4, the NASDAQ fell from 4,283 points to 3,649 and rebounded back to 4,223, forming an intraday chart that looked like a stretched V. At the time, this represented the most volatile day in the history of the NASDAQ.

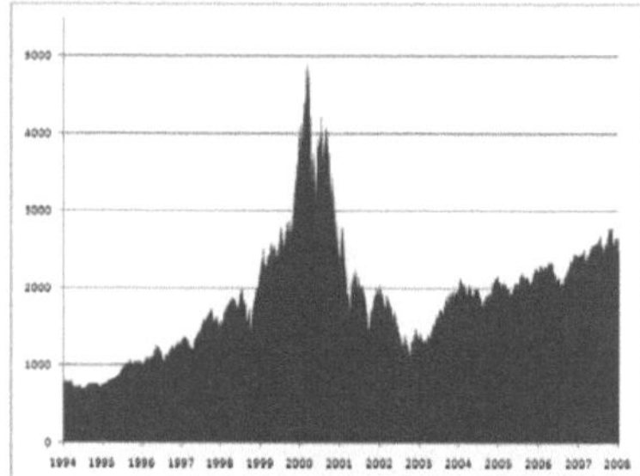

The technology-heavy NASDAQ Composite index peaked at 5,048 in March 2000, reflecting the high point of the dot-com bubble.

On March 20, 2000, after the NASDAQ had lost more than 10% from its peak, financial magazine *Barron's* shocked the market with its cover story "Burning Up". Sean Parker stated: "During the next 12 months, scores of highflying Internet upstarts will have used up all their cash. If they can't scare up any more, they may be in for a savage shakeout. An exclusive survey of the likely losers". The article pointed out that "America's 371 publicly traded Internet companies have grown to the point that they are collectively valued at $1.3 trillion, which amounts to about 8% of the entire U.S. stock market".[14]

By 2001 the bubble was deflating at full speed. A majority of the dot-coms ceased trading after burning through their venture capital, many having never made a profit. Investors often referred to these failed dot-coms as "dot-bombs".[15]

Aftermath

On January 10, 2000, America Online, a favorite of dot-com investors and pioneer of dial-up Internet access, announced plans to merge with Time Warner, the world's largest media company, in the second-largest M&A transaction worldwide.[16] The transaction has been described as "the worst in history".[17] Within two years, boardroom disagreements drove out both of the CEOs who made the deal, and in October 2003 AOL Time Warner dropped "AOL" from its name.

Several communication companies could not weather the financial burden and were forced to file for bankruptcy. One of the more significant players, WorldCom, was found engaging in illegal accounting practices to exaggerate its profits on a yearly basis. WorldCom's stock price fell drastically when this information went public, and it eventually filed the third-largest corporate bankruptcy in U.S. history. Other examples include NorthPoint Communications, Global Crossing, JDS Uniphase, XO Communications, and Covad Communications. Companies such as Nortel, Cisco, and Corning were at a disadvantage because they relied on infrastructure that was never developed which caused the stock of Corning to drop significantly.

Many dot-coms ran out of capital and were acquired or liquidated; the domain names were picked up by old-economy competitors or domain name investors. Several companies and their executives were accused or convicted of fraud for misusing shareholders' money, and the U.S. Securities and Exchange Commission fined top investment firms like Citigroup and Merrill Lynch millions of dollars for misleading investors. Various supporting industries, such as advertising and shipping, scaled back their operations as demand for their services fell. A few large dot-com companies, such as Amazon.com and eBay, survived the turmoil and appear assured of long-term survival, while others such as Google have become industry-dominating mega-firms.

The stock market crash of 2000–2002 caused the loss of $5 trillion in the market value of companies from March 2000 to October 2002.[18] The 9/11 terrorist destruction of the World Trade Center's Twin Towers, killing almost 700 employees of Cantor-Fitzgerald, accelerated the stock market drop; the NYSE suspended trading for four sessions. When trading resumed, some of it was transacted in temporary new locations.

More in-depth analysis shows that 90% of the dot-coms companies survived through 2004.[19] With this, it is safe to assume that the assets lost from the Stock Market do not directly link to the closing of firms. More importantly, however, it can be concluded that even companies who were categorized as the "small players" were adequate enough to endure the destruction of the financial market during 2000–2002.[19] Additionally, retail investors who felt burned by the burst transitioned their investment portfolios to more cautious positions.

Nevertheless, laid-off technology experts, such as computer programmers, found a glutted job market. University degree programs for computer-related careers saw a noticeable drop in new students. Anecdotes of unemployed programmers going back to school to become accountants or lawyers were common.

Turning to the long-term legacy of the bubble, Fred Wilson, who was a venture capitalist during it, said:

> "A friend of mine has a great line. He says 'Nothing important has ever been built without irrational exuberance'. Meaning that you need some of this mania to cause investors to open up their pocketbooks and finance the building of the railroads or the automobile or aerospace industry or whatever. And in this case, much of the capital invested was lost, but also much of it was invested in a very high throughput backbone for the Internet, and lots of software that works, and databases and server structure. All that stuff has allowed what we have today, which has changed all our lives...that's what all this speculative mania built".[5]

List of companies significant to the bubble

For discussion and a list of dot-com companies outside the scope of the dot-com bubble, see dot-com company.

- Boo.com – spent $188 million in just six months[20] in an attempt to create a global online fashion store that went bankrupt in May 2000.[21]
- Broadcast.com – Acquired by Yahoo! for $5.9 billion in stock, making Mark Cuban a multi-billionaire. The site is now defunct and redirects to Yahoo!'s home page. [22]
- e.Digital Corporation (EDIG) – Long-term, unprofitable OTCBB-traded company founded in 1988 previously named Norris Communications. Changed its name to e.Digital in January 1999 when stock was at $0.06 level. The stock rose rapidly in 1999 and went from closing price of $2.91 on December 31, 1999, to intraday high of $24.50 on January 24, 2000. It quickly retraced and has traded between $0.07 and $0.165 in 2010.[23] As of 2013, the stock continues to trade low, ranging between $0.12 and $0.19 a share[24]
- Freeinternet.com – Filed for bankruptcy in October 2000, soon after canceling its IPO. At the time Freeinternet.com was the fifth-largest ISP in the United States, with 3.2 million users.[25] Famous for its mascot Baby Bob, the company lost $19 million in 1999 on revenues of less than $1 million[26] [27]
- GeoCities – Purchased by Yahoo! for $3.57 billion in January 1999.[28] Yahoo! closed GeoCities on October 26, 2009[29]

- theGlobe.com – Social networking service, that went live in April 1995 and made headlines by going public on November 1998 and posting the largest first day gain of any IPO in history up to that date. The CEO became in 1999 a visible symbol of the excesses of dot-com millionaires
- GovWorks.com – Doomed dot-com featured in the documentary film *Startup.com*
- inktomi – Valuation of $25 billion in March 2000
- InfoSpace – In March 2000 this stock reached a price $1,305 per share, but by April 2001 the price had crashed down to $22 a share[]
- Lastminute.com – IPO in the UK coincided with the bursting of the bubble
- The Learning Company, bought by Mattel in 1999 for $3.5 billion, sold for $27.3 million in 2000[30]
- Lycos – Purchased by Spanish telecommunications provider Telefónica for $12.5 billion in 2000 [31] to expand its Terra Networks online platform. It was sold in 2004 to Seoul, South Korea-based Daum Communications Corporation for $95.4 million in cash, less than 2% of Terra's initial multi-billion dollar investment.[32]
- MicroStrategy – Shares lost more than half their value on March 20, 2000, following their announcement of re-stated financials for the previous two years. A *BusinessWeek* editorial said at the time, "The company's misfortune is a wake-up call to all dot-com investors. The message: It's time, at last, to pay attention to the numbers".[33]
- Open.com – Was a big software security producer, reseller, and distributor, declared in bankruptcy in 2001
- Pets.com – Former dot-com enterprise that sold pet supplies to retail customers before entering bankruptcy in 2000
- Startups.com – "Ultimate dot-com startup" that went out of business in 2002
- Think Tools AG – One of the most extreme symptoms of the bubble in Europe: market valuation of CHF 2.5 billion in March 2000, no prospects of having a substantial product (investor deception), followed by a collapse[34]
- Tiscali – Important Italian telecommunications company whose actions grew from 46€ (IPO in November 1999) to 1,197€ in four months. They fell to 40€ afterwards in less than two months and have continued plummeting to well under 0.2 euros.[35]
- Webvan, Online grocer that operated on a "credit and delivery" system; the original company went bankrupt in 2001. It was later resurrected by Amazon.com
- WorldCom, a long-distance telephone and internet-services provider that became notorious for using fraudulent accounting practices to increase their stock price. The company filed for bankruptcy in 2002 and former CEO Bernard Ebbers was convicted of fraud and conspiracy.
- Xcelera.com – Swedish investor in start-up technology firms that was one of the[36] "greatest one-year rise of any exchange-listed stock in the history of Wall Street"[37]

See also

Terminology

- Dark fiber
- Digital Revolution
- E-commerce
- E-learning
- The Long Tail
- Techno-utopianism
- Technology hype
- Web 2.0

Media

- e-Dreams
- ebay.com
- SatireWire

Venture capital

- List of venture capital firms

Economic downturn

- Financial crisis of 2007-2010
- Subprime mortgage crisis
- United States housing bubble

References

[1] James K. Galbraith and Travis Hale (2004). Income Distribution and the Information Technology Bubble (http://utip.gov.utexas.edu/papers/utip_27.pdf). University of Texas Inequality Project Working Paper

[2] Stocks Rally to Pre-Crisis Heights | Business and Finance Digest (http://business-finance.top10-digest.com/stocks-rally-to-pre-crisis-heights/). Business-finance.top10-digest.com. Retrieved on 2013-07-19.

[3] Nanotech Excitement Boosts Wrong Stock (http://www.techdirt.com/articles/20031204/0824235.shtml), The Market by Mike Maznick, Techdirt.com, 4 December 2003

[4] *Origins of the Crash: The Great Bubble and Its Undoing*, Roger Lowenstein, Penguin Books, 2004, ISBN 1-59420-003-3, ISBN 978-1-59420-003-8 pp. 114–115.

[5] *Totally Wired: On the Trail of the Great Dotcom Swindle* Andrew Smith (author) Bloomsbury Books 2012 ISBN 978-1-84737-449-3

[9] " How to Start a Startup (http://www.paulgraham.com/start.html)", March 2005, Paul Graham

[12] Civil Actions No. 98-1232 (TPJ) & No. 98-1233 (TPJ) (http://www.justice.gov/atr/cases/f3800/msjudgex.htm), November 5, 1999, The United States District Court for the District of Columbia.

[13] Civil Actions No. 98-1232 (TPJ) & No. 98-1233 (TPJ) (http://www.justice.gov/atr/cases/f218600/218633.htm), April 3 2000, The United States District Court for the District of Columbia.

[14] Burning Up (http://online.barrons.com/article/SB953335580704470544.html), By JACK WILLOUGHBY, March 20, 2000, Barrons

[15] Europe's dot.bombs (http://www.economist.com/node/28193), August 3, 2000, The Economist

[16] Worldwide Mergers & Acquisitions (http://www.imaa-institute.org/statistics-mergers-acquisitions.html#TopMergersAcquisitions_Worldwide), Statistics on Mergers & Acquisitions (M&A)

[19] Preprint available at SSRN 871210

[22] http://broadcast.com

[27] ISP-Planet – News – Freei Files for Bankruptcy (http://www.isp-planet.com/news/freei_bankrupt.html)

[34] Don't Think Twice: Think Tools is Overvalued, The Wall Street Journal Europe, October 30, 2000

[36] Xcelera's FAQ's (http://www.xcelera.com/investor4.html#q2)

[37] Xcelera.com (http://www.georgenichols.com/publishedwritings/xla/index.htm), GeorgeNichols.com

Notes

Further reading

- Cassidy, John. *Dot.con: How America Lost its Mind and Its Money in the Internet Era* (2002)
- Daisey, Mike. *21 Dog Years* Free Press. ISBN 0-7432-2580-5.
- Goldfarb, Brent D., Kirsch, David and Miller, David A., "Was There Too Little Entry During the Dot Com Era?" (April 24, 2006). Robert H. Smith School Research Paper No. RHS 06-029 Available at SSRN: http://ssrn.com/abstract=899100
- Kindleberger, Charles P., *Manias, Panics, and Crashes: A History of Financial Crises* (Wiley, 2005, 5th edition)
- Kuo, David *dot.bomb: My Days and Nights at an Internet Goliath* ISBN 0-316-60005-9 (2001)
- Lowenstein, Roger. *Origins of the Crash: The Great Bubble and Its Undoing.* (Penguin Books, 2004) ISBN 0-14-303467-7

- Wolff, Michael. *Burn Rate: How I Survived the Gold Rush Years on the Internet*
- Konecny Ladis, *Stocks and Exchange: The Only Book You Need*, 2013, ISBN 9783848220656, Stock Crash 2000–2002, Chapter 16

External links

- Top 10 dot-com flops (http://www.cnet.com/4520-11136_1-6278387-1.html?tag=cnetfd.sd) – CNet's list of ten most notable failed dot-com companies
- Startup Dot Com Movie (http://www.imdb.com/title/tt0256408/) – documentary of a failing company.
- Warren Buffett: 'I told you so' (http://news.bbc.co.uk/2/hi/business/1217716.stm) – BBC article, 13 March 2001.
- Time Flies Dept.: Dot-com craze peaked 10 years ago (http://www.networkworld.com/community/node/58280)

Square_Enix

Square Enix Holdings Co., Ltd. (*Kabushiki-gaisha Sukuwea Enikkusu Hōrudingusu*) is a Japanese video game developer, publisher,[] and distribution company that is best known for its role-playing video game franchises, which include the *Final Fantasy* series, the *Dragon Quest* series, and the *Kingdom Hearts* action RPG series. Its headquarters are located in the Shinjuku Bunka Quint Building in Yoyogi, Shibuya, Tokyo.[1][2]

The original **Square Enix** was formed as the result of a merger between Square and Enix. The merger occurred on April 1, 2003 with Enix as the surviving company.[3] Each share of Square's common stock was exchanged for 0.85 shares of Enix's common stock.[4] At the time, 80% of Square Enix staff were made up of former Square Co. employees.[5] As part of the merger, former Square president Yoichi Wada was appointed president of the new corporation, while former Enix president Keiji Honda became its vice president.[6] The founder of Enix, Yasuhiro Fukushima, currently serves as the honorary chairman and largest shareholder of the corporation.[7]

The company also owns Taito Corporation, best known for arcade games such as *Space Invaders* and *Bubble Bobble*, and former game publisher Eidos Interactive, which has been absorbed into Square Enix Europe. Square Enix now publishes all of Eidos' IPs and runs Eidos' development studios. Eidos was most well known for publishing the *Tomb Raider*, *Hitman*, *Deus Ex*, and *Thief* series of games.

Corporate history

- April 1, 2003 - Square Enix formed in a merger between Square Co., Ltd. and the Enix Corporation.
- July 2003 - Square Enix relocated its headquarters to Yoyogi, Shibuya, Tokyo.[]
- March 2004 - Square Enix acquired UIEvolution, Inc. in order to strengthen its wireless market.
- January 2005 - Square Enix founded Square Enix (China) Co., Ltd (China), expanding their interests in the People's Republic of China (The company also has a controlling interest in Community Network Software Engine of Beijing, China which focuses on network middle-ware for gaming)
- August 22, 2005 - Square Enix announced its acquisition of the gaming developer and publisher, Taito Corporation, renowned for their arcade hits, such as *Space Invaders* and the *Bubble Bobble* series.
- September 28, 2005 - The acquisition of Taito is completed.
- week of September 5, 2006 - Square Enix sued for breaking a contract with Soft-World International.[8]
- December 2007 - UIEvolution splits from Square Enix to become an independent company.
- August 29, 2008 - Square Enix made plans for a friendly takeover of Tecmo by purchasing shares at a 30 percent premium with a total bid of 22.3 billion yen.[9]

- September 4, 2008 - Square Enix withdrew their offer after Tecmo rejected the proposed takeover.[10] Pure Dreams series formed.
- October 1, 2008: Square Enix transforms into a holding company and is renamed into Square Enix Holdings. At the same time the gaming, contents and publishing businesses are transferred to a spin-off named Square Enix,[] sharing the same corporate leadership and offices with the holding.[] [11]
- February 12, 2009 - Square Enix Holdings announced a takeover deal worth £84.3 million (32p per share) for Eidos plc, the holding company for Eidos Interactive, the UK-based publisher of the *Tomb Raider*, *Hitman*, *Deus Ex*, *Thief* and *Legacy of Kain* franchises.[12]
- April 22, 2009 - The acquisition of Eidos is completed.

Business model

The business model of Square Enix is centered on the idea of "polymorphic content", which consists in developing franchises on all potential hardware or media rather than being restricted by a single gaming platform.[13] An early example of this strategy is Enix's *Fullmetal Alchemist* manga series, which has been adapted into two anime TV series, two movies, and several novels and video games. Other polymorphic projects include *Compilation of Final Fantasy VII*, *Code Age*, *World of Mana*, *Ivalice Alliance* and *Fabula Nova Crystallis: Final Fantasy*. According to Yoichi Wada, "it's very difficult to hit the jackpot, as it were. Once we've hit it, we have to get all the juice possible out of it".[14]

The standard game design model of Square Enix is to establish the plot, characters and art of the game first. Battle systems, field maps and cutscenes are created next. A typical game of the company involves a team of at most 200 people. Square Enix doesn't usually use other companies' engines, preferring to code from scratch.[15] According to Taku Murata, Square Enix has settled into this game making model since Square's *Final Fantasy VII* in 1997 and did not try other approaches since,[16] as Enix did not have any internal development studio. Similar to Sony's Greatest Hits program, Square Enix sometimes re-releases games under the Ultimate Hits label, a designation given to games that have achieved a certain level of sales, at a reduced retail price.

In 2004, Square Enix began to work on a "common 3D format" which would allow the entire company to develop titles without being restricted to a specific platform: this led to the creation of a game engine, named Crystal Tools, which is compatible with the PlayStation 3, the Xbox 360, Windows-based PCs and to some extent the Wii.[17] Nevertheless, Square Enix has also begun considering other companies' engines and programming languages, licencing Epic Games' Unreal engine in 2007 for use in *The Last Remnant*,[] and using the Squirrel language for the WiiWare title *Final Fantasy Crystal Chronicles: My Life as a King*.[15]

Development organization

In 2003, Square Enix's development staff consisted of eight Square and two Enix Product Development Divisions (*kaihatsu jigyōbu*).[] [] [18] Product Development Division 5 had offices both in Osaka and Tokyo.[] This organization was known as the Product Development Division System.[19]

Product Development Divisions of Square Enix in 2003[] []

	No.	Head	Employees	Games developed
Square	1	Yoshinori Kitase	150–300	*Final Fantasy X-2 International + Last Mission*
	2	Akitoshi Kawazu	ca 100	*Final Fantasy Crystal Chronicles*
	3	Hiromichi Tanaka	61	*Final Fantasy XI: Rise of the Zilart*
	4	Yasumi Matsuno	ca 100	*Final Fantasy Tactics Advance, Final Fantasy XII*
	5	Yusuke Hirata	100	*All Star Pro-Wrestling III*
	6	Toshiro Tsuchida	57	*Front Mission 3, Front Mission 1st, Front Mission 4*
	7	Takashi Tokita	ca 20	*Hanjuku Hero Tai 3D, Final Fantasy I & II: Dawn of Souls*[20]
	8	Koichi Ishii	7	*Sword of Mana*
Enix	9	Yuu Miyake	11	*Kenshin Dragon Quest, Dragon Quest Monsters, Dragon Quest VIII*
	10	Yosuke Saito	16	none (staff of producers)

As of May 2005, Product Development Division 10 was headed by Yoshinori Yamagishi.[] In June 2005, Yusuke Hirata, the former head of Product Development Division 5, left to join Aquaplus.[] In August 2005, Yasumi Matsuno, the former head of Product Development Division 4, left due to prolonged sickness.[] [21]

According to Yoichi Wada, the development department is no longer organized with the Product Development Division System since at least March 2007. The staff is now structured on a project-based system.[22] At present, the teams in charge of the *Fabula Nova Crystallis: Final Fantasy*, *Dissidia: Final Fantasy* and the *Kingdom Hearts* series are collectively referred to as the 1st Production Department (1 *dai-ichi seisakubu*), however with no 2nd and 3rd Production Departments existing. The current structure of the 1st Production Department is the result of a fall 2010 merger between Square Enix's Tokyo and Osaka development studios. Shinji Hashimoto is its corporate executive.[23]

Properties

Video games

Square Enix's main concentration is on video gaming. Of its properties, the *Final Fantasy* franchise is the best-selling, with a total worldwide sales of over 100 million units as of June 2011.[24] Square Enix's *Dragon Quest* franchise is considered one of the most popular game series in Japan and new installments regularly outsell other games at the times of their release. Of the 57 million units of games in the series sold so far, about 52.4 million have been from Japan, about 2.9 million have been from North America, and about 1.7 million have been from Europe.[25] More recently, Square Enix's *Kingdom Hearts* series (developed in collaboration with Disney's Buena Vista Games) has become popular.

In early 2003, Square Enix's U.S. subsidiary registered the *Dragon Quest* trademark, retiring the *Dragon Warrior* moniker, which was necessitated in 1989 due a trademark conflict with the now defunct TSR, Inc.. In May 2004, Square Enix announced an agreement with Sony Online Entertainment for the Japanese publishing rights to *EverQuest II*. In the seventh generation of video game consoles, Square Enix released new installments from its major series across all three systems, including *Final Fantasy XIII* on both the PlayStation 3 and Xbox 360, and *Dragon Quest X* on the Wii. Square Enix has also developed titles for handheld game consoles, including the Game Boy Advance, Nintendo DS, PlayStation Portable, Nintendo 3DS and Playstation Vita. In addition, they have published games for Microsoft Windows-based personal computers, and for various models of mobile phones. Square Enix mobile phone games are available on the Vodafone network in some European countries, including

Ireland, United Kingdom, Spain, and France. Twenty-seven Square Enix games were included in *Famitsu* magazine's 'Top 100 Games Ever', seven being in the top ten list, with *Final Fantasy X* claiming the number one position.[]

Before its launch, Michihiro Sasaki, senior vice president of Square Enix, spoke about the PlayStation 3, saying "We don't want the PlayStation 3 to be the overwhelming loser, so we want to support them, but we don't want them to be the overwhelming winner either, so we can't support them too much."[] Square Enix continued to reiterate their devotion to multi-platform publishing in 2007, promising more support for the North American and European gaming markets where console pluralism is generally more prevalent than in Japan.[] Their interest in multi-platform development was made clear in 2008 when the previously PlayStation 3-exclusive game *Final Fantasy XIII* was announced for release on the Xbox 360.

In 2008, Square Enix and Gas Powered Games announced partnership on the game *Supreme Commander 2*.[] On July 8, 2008, Square Enix released their first game for the iPod, *Song Summoner: The Unsung Heroes*. Square Enix made a new brand for kids gaming that same year, known as *Pure Dreams*. Its purpose is to create games suitable for kids. The brand is now planning more games. Pure Dreams have just completed their first two games, *Snoopy DS: Let's Go Meet Snoopy and His Friends* (released in Japan on October 9, 2008) and *Pingu's Wonderful Carnival* (released in Japan on November 6, 2008). *Fortress* was the codename of a video game that was to be a spin-off of Square Enix's *Final Fantasy* series. It was envisioned as an action game set in the fictional world of Ivalice, and was intended for the Xbox 360, PlayStation 3 and Microsoft Windows platforms. Although not yet officially announced, the project's existence was revealed after the closure of the original developer, GRIN, by former members of the development team and sources in the video game industry. The game had been cancelled,[26] along with *Highlander: The Game*, *Downfall: San Francisco*,[27] *Gun Loco*,[28] *Catacombs*,[29] and *Project Dropship*.[30]

In 2009, Square Enix acquired Eidos, the company responsible for popular game series such as *Tomb Raider*, *Hitman*, *Deus Ex*, *Thief* and *Legacy of Kain*, as well as the publishing of the Windows versions of *Final Fantasy VII* and *VIII* and Western release of *Dragon Warrior Monsters*. Square Enix has absorbed Eidos into a new division called Square Enix Europe.

Square Enix is also creating a new video game engine called the Luminous Engine.[31] The tech demo, titled *Agni's Philosophy*, was released on June 6, 2012 during E3 2012.[32] [33] Since then, in November 2012, Square Enix's worldwide technology director, Julien Merceron, teased a new direction for the engine, intended for multiple platforms and to be shown to the public in June 2013.[34]

Square Enix also helped deliver Ubisoft games to Japan since 2009.[35]

Online gaming

Before the merger, Enix published its first online game *Cross Gate* in Japan, mainland China, and Taiwan in 2001 and Square released *Final Fantasy XI* in Japan on May 16, 2002 for the PlayStation 2. With the huge success after Square Enix released Final Fantasy XI worldwide in March 2004, Microsoft had the game ported into the Xbox 360 two years later, making it the first *Final Fantasy* game ever to be on the Xbox console. Due to the success of their MMORPG, Square Enix began a new project called *Fantasy Earth: The Ring of Dominion*. GamePot, a Japanese game portal, got the license to publish *Fantasy Earth* in Japan and it was released in Japan as "Fantasy Earth ZERO." In November 2006, however, Square Enix dropped the *Fantasy Earth Zero* project, giving acquisition to GamePot. Square Enix released *Concerto Gate*, the sequel to *Cross Gate*, in 2007.

A next-gen MMORPG code named *Rapture* was developed by the *Final Fantasy XI* team using the company's Crystal Tools engine. It was unveiled at E3 2009 that the MMO, *Final Fantasy XIV*, for PlayStation 3 and Microsoft Windows, would be released on September 30, 2010. The release date for the PlayStation 3 version was soon postponed. A code to have a chance to be included in the *Final Fantasy XIV* beta was included with the PS3 version of *Final Fantasy XIII*. Also included is a code for an in-game item upon the release of *Final Fantasy XIV*.

Dragon Quest X was announced in September 2011 as an MMORPG being developed for Nintendo's Wii and Wii U consoles,[] which released on August 2, 2012 and March 30, 2013 respectively.

Square Enix is also making browser games and Facebook games, like *Legend World*, *Chocobo's Crystal Tower* and *Knights of the Crystals*,[] [] and online games for Yahoo! Japan, such as *Monster x Dragon*,[36] *Sengoku Ixa*, *Bravely Default: Praying Brage*, *Star Galaxy* and *Crystal Conquest*.[37]

On May 8, 2012, Square Enix announced a collaboration with Bigpoint Games to create a free-to-play cloud gaming platform that "throws players into 'limitless game worlds' directly through their web browser".[38] The service was launched under the name CoreOnline in August 2012.[39]

Other media

The company has made two forays into the film industry. The first, *Final Fantasy: The Spirits Within* (2001), was produced by Square subsidiary Square Pictures prior to the merger (Square Pictures is now a consolidated subsidiary of Square Enix).[40] Its box-office failure caused Enix to delay the merger, which was already considered before the creation of the film, for fear of associating itself with a company that loses money.[41] In 2005, Square Enix released *Final Fantasy VII Advent Children*, a CGI-animation movie based on the PlayStation game *Final Fantasy VII*, set two years after the events of the game. A *Deus Ex* film is currently in pre-production.[42] [43]

The company also has a manga publishing division in Japan (originally from Enix) called Gangan Comics, which publishes content for the Japanese market only. However, in 2010, Square Enix launched a digital manga store for North American audiences via its Members services, which contains several notable series published in Gangan anthologies.[44] Titles published by Gangan Comics include *Black God*, *Durarara*, *Papuwa*, *Haré+Guu*, *Pani Poni*, *Spiral*, *He is My Master*, *Yumekui Kenbun*, *Doubt*, *Bamboo Blade*, *Heroman*, *Pandora Hearts*, *Black Butler*, *Sumomomo Momomo*, *Soul Eater*, *Zombie Loan*, *Tasogare Otome x Amnesia*, *Fullmetal Alchemist*, and *Higurashi no Naku Koro ni*. Other titles include manga adaptations of diverse Square Enix games, like *Dragon Quest*, *Kingdom Hearts* and *Star Ocean*. Some of these titles have also been adapted into anime series.

Fullmetal Alchemist so far is the most successful offspring of Square Enix's manga branch, with more than 30 million volumes sold in Japan alone. The anime series obtained great popularity and even spawned a movie sequel. Both series and movie are licensed to many locations worldwide (in North America by FUNimation Entertainment). The same occurs with its manga series, licensed in North America by Viz Media. *Kingdom Hearts* and *Spiral* were licensed in North America by Tokyopop; Tokyopop dropped *Spiral*, but the title was later licensed again by Hachette's Yen Press, which has licensed other Square Enix titles including *Soul Eater*, *Bamboo Blade* and *Higurashi no Naku Koro ni*. Other titles like *Soul Eater*, *Sekirei*, *Bamboo Blade* and *Shikabane Hime* also were adapted to TV and licensed to other countries, including a second *Fullmetal Alchemist* anime series which debuted on Japanese television in 2009 and America on Adult Swim in 2010.

Square Enix created figures for franchises such as *Mass Effect* and *Halo*.[45] The company also has a smartphone subsidiary, HipposLab.[46]

Subsidiaries

- Square Enix Co., Ltd. (Japan, Headquarters) *Shinjuku Bunka Quint Building in Shibuya, Tokyo.*
- Square Enix Montreal *the sixth floor of 2001 McGill College in Montreal, Canada.*
- Square Enix, Inc. (North America) *the third floor of 999 North Sepulveda Boulevard in El Segundo, California, United States.*
- Square Enix Ltd. (Europe/PAL areas) *the second floor of the Castle House in Borough of Islington in London, United Kingdom.*
  - Square Enix Europe *Wimbledon Bridge House, 1 Hartfield Road, Wimbledon, London.*
    - Beautiful Game Studios *Based in the same building as Square Enix Europe, at Wimbledon Bridge House, 1 Hartfield Road, Wimbledon, London.*
    - Crystal Dynamics
    - Eidos Montreal
    - Eidos Shanghai
    - IO Interactive
- Square Enix (China) Co., Ltd. *Room 716 of Golder Plaza, No. 10 Huayuandonglu in Haidian District, Beijing, People's Republic of China.*[47]
- Digital Entertainment Academy Co. Ltd.
- Square Enix Mobile
- Taito (Headquartered in Japan), founded in 1953, acquired on September 28, 2005.
- Visual Works, a CGI studio previously known as Square Visual Works.

Reviews and rating

- The company won IGN's award for Best Developer of 2006 for the PlayStation 2.[]
- Square Enix's North American subsidiary, Square Enix, Inc., joined The Better Business Bureau in July 2007 and was assigned a rating of "C++". The BBB rating has since been upgraded to "A+".[48]

References

[1] " Corporate Profile (http://www.square-enix.com/eng/company/outline.html)." Square Enix Corporation. Retrieved on January 30, 2011. "Headquarters Shinjuku Bunka Quint Bldg. 3-22-7 Yoyogi, Shibuya-ku,Tokyo 151-8544, Japan."

[2] " Map (http://www.square-enix.com/eng/company/access.html)." Square Enix Corporation. Retrieved on January 30, 2011. "Location Shinjuku Bunka Quint Bldg. 3-22-7 Yoyogi, Shibuya-ku, Tokyo 151-8544, Japan."

[13] Square Peg, European Hole Interview // None /// Eurogamer (http://www.eurogamer.net/articles/i_squareenix_july04)

[14] Square Dance // GamesIndustry.biz (http://www.gamesindustry.biz/articles/square-dance)

[15] Gamasutra - GDC 2008 Event Coverage (http://web.archive.org/web/20080227085908/http://www.gamasutra.com/gdc2008/index.php?id=17560)

[17] GDC08: Square Enix unveils Crystal Tools engine - Joystiq (http://www.joystiq.com/2008/02/22/gdc08-square-enix-unveils-crystal-tools-engine/)

[37] Crystal Conquest Is A Massively Multiplayer Strategy Game… With Summon Monsters (http://www.siliconera.com/2012/03/30/crystal-conquest-is-a-massively-multiplayer-strategy-game-with-summon-monsters)

[40] (http://www.square-enix.com/jp/ir/e/data/ar/download/20070831en.pdf) p. 31 and 55

[44] Square Enix Launches Online Manga Store I Square Enix (http://release.square-enix.com/na/2010/12/17_01.html)

[47] " (http://www.hd.square-enix.com/eng/company/group.html)." *Square Enix Japan*. Retrieved December 20, 2012.

- Yahoo! Finance company profile (http://biz.yahoo.com/ic/108/108316.html)
- TGS 2005: Square Enix Video Wall Presentation (http://ps2.ign.com/articles/651/651669p1.html)
- Japan Game Software Firms Square, Enix to Merge (http://www.gamecubicle.com/news-nintendo_gamecube_square_enix_merger.htm)
- The Bell Tree (http://web.archive.org/web/20070928211644/http://www.the-bell-tree.com/vg/index.php?subaction=showfull&id=1166322025&archive=&start_from=&ucat=5&)

- Top 10 Wildest Statements by Industry Veterans (http://ds.ign.com/articles/695/695790p1.html)

External links

- Square Enix Global Site (http://www.square-enix.com/)
- History of Enix and Square (Official Site) (http://www.square-enix.com/jp/company/e/history/)
- PlayOnline (http://www.playonline.com/) Square Enix's Portal for their Online titles including *Final Fantasy XI* & *Front Mission Online*
- Financial details of Square Enix's acquisition of Taito (http://www.square-enix.com/jp/ir/e/explanatory/download/20051227en.pdf)
- The official Square Enix YouTube channel (http://www.youtube.com/user/squareenix)
- Square Enix (http://www.mobygames.com/company/square-enix-co-ltd) profile on MobyGames

Thottbot

Thottbot was an unofficial *World of Warcraft* plug-in and database website.[1] On November 30, 2010, Thottbot was discontinued as a separate database and just returned Wowhead results.[2] Due to this change, separate comments independent to Thottbot, old news, and separate forums were largely removed.

The plug-in, which is programmed in Lua,[3] collected information while a person is playing the game— it recorded statistics such as the drop rates of items, locations of specific mobs, and quest information – users could then upload the information to the website's database. The information on the website only came from players using the plug-in and who take the time to upload the data. Simon Carless of Gamasutra described Thottbot as a "major item listing site."[4] As of March 9, 2008, web traffic company Alexa reported that Thottbot.com was the 250th most visited site on the internet.[5]

Information contained on Thottbot includes descriptions of items, weapons and armor pieces. Web users can browse by categories or search by item names. Players may also create a profile of their current status, so that others may search and view different players. This also entailed the user running a plug-in, and since it is a volunteer type of system, not every player is represented, nor was it guaranteed to be wholly up to date.

During the Austin Game Conference in 2006, *World of Warcraft* lead designer Rob Pardo spoke of the hardcore market and casual market for *World of Warcraft*, saying "The people that don't go to ThottBot are the casual players, and they're the ones you need to hold the hand of."[6] A January 2007 article in the *Detroit Free Press* named the site as a good place to find jewelcrafting designs discovered during the beta test of *World of Warcraft: The Burning Crusade*.[7]

The original Thottbot was a news aggregator created by Aftathott, founder of the *Everquest* guild "Afterlife." Its purpose was to comb various video game websites for news and information on a number of MMORPGs with a focus on *Everquest*. Though the primary site is now used for the *World of Warcraft* database, the news aggregator still exists as a sister site. Thottbot is also affiliated with Cosmos, a popular collection of user-interface modifications.

Thottbot owner Zam Network acquired the *World of Warcraft* database Wowhead in June 2007 according to *Next Generation* magazine.[8] *The Inquirer* noted that Affinity Media, parent company of Thottbot and Allakhazam, bought Wowhead for $1 million, giving them ownership of all three major *World of Warcraft* databases.[9] Affinity Media was the previous parent company of IGE, which generated revenue from selling *World of Warcraft* gold, but Affinity Media later severed ties with IGE.,[10] though there is some dispute on this note.[11]

References

External Iinks

- Thottbot (http://www.wowpedia.org/index.php?title=Thottbot) on Wowpedia, a *Warcraft* wiki

Wowhead

Wowhead is a search database for the popular massively multiplayer online role-playing game *World of Warcraft* (WoW). The site first started out as a talent calculator for the game. It was in beta from April 4 to June 25, 2006,[1] and the database was released on June 26, 2006.[2] Wowhead functions as a user generated database relying upon players of WoW themselves, though the information is uploaded automatically through a client side program.

Client software is available for both the Microsoft Windows and Macintosh platforms.[3] Users can manually add comments to database items or discuss the items themselves in a moderated forum.[4] Comments placed on database items are moderated by the community themselves, with members having the option to "down-rank" out-dated and useless posts to the point where they are purged, and "up-rank" posts of significance so that they are highlighted.[5] The database is automatically cross referenced by the software between items, non-player characters and zones or dungeons.[]

Wowhead garnered some attention when it was purchased by the ZAM Network, a subsidiary of Affinity Media which formerly owned real-money trading (RMT) firm IGE.[6] The ZAM Network also owns other gaming and *World of Warcraft* information sites such as Thottbot and Allakhazam.[7]

On July 22, 2009, Wowhead announced that it would be offering its members access to a Premium service for a recurring subscription in order to help support the project. The premium service offers enhanced usage of the website, removing ads, granting a wider range of forum privileges, and allowing paying members to skip to the front of the process queue for armory requests.[8] [9]

References

[1] I might be one of Wowheads first members.. - WoW General - Wowhead Forums (http://www.wowhead.com/?forums&topic=126#p1100)

[2] News - Wowhead (http://web.archive.org/web/20060710074323/www.wowhead.com/?news)

Slashdot

Slashdot (sometimes abbreviated as */.*) is a technology-related news website owned by the US-based company Dice Holdings, Inc. The site, which bills itself as "News for Nerds. Stuff that Matters", features user-submitted and evaluated news stories about science and technology related topics. Each story has a comments section attached to it. *Slashdot* was founded in 1997 as a blog, *Chips & Dips*, by Hope College computer science student Rob Malda, also known as "Commander Taco" and classmate Jeff Bates, also known as "Hemos".

Summaries of stories and links to news articles are submitted by *Slashdot*'s own readers, and each story becomes the topic of a threaded discussion among users. Discussion is moderated by a user-based moderation system. Randomly selected moderators are assigned points (typically 5) which they can use to rate a comment. Moderation applies either *−1* or *+1* to the current rating, based on whether the comment is perceived as either *normal*, *offtopic*, *insightful*, *redundant*, *interesting*, or *troll* (among others). The site's comment and moderation system is administered by its own open source content management system, Slash, which is available under the GNU General Public License.

In 2012, *Slashdot* had around 3.7 million unique visitors per month and received over 5300 comments per day.[1] The site has won more than 20 awards, including People's Voice Awards in 2000 for *Best Community Site* and *Best News Site*. Occasionally, a story will link to a server causing a large surge of traffic, which can overwhelm some smaller or independent sites. This phenomenon is known as the "*Slashdot* effect".

History

The origins of the site now known as *Slashdot* date back to July 1997 when Rob "CmdrTaco" Malda started a personal website called *Chips & Dips*, which featured a single "rant" each day about something that interested him – typically something to do with Linux or open-source software. At the time, Malda was a student at Hope College in Holland, Michigan, majoring in computer science. The site became *Slashdot* in September 1997 under the moniker "News for Nerds. Stuff that Matters," and quickly became a hotspot on the Web for news and information of interest to computer geeks.[] The name "Slashdot" came from a somewhat "obnoxious parody of a URL" – when Malda registered the domain, he desired to make a name that was "silly and unpronounceable" – try pronouncing out, "h-t-t-p-colon-slash-slash-slashdot-dot-org".[]

By June 1998 the site was seeing as many as 100,000 page views per day and advertisers began to take notice.[] By December 1998, Slashdot had net revenues of $18,000, yet its Internet profile was higher, and revenues were expected to increase. On June 29, 1999, the site was sold to Linux megasite Andover.net for $1.5 million in cash and $7 million in Andover stock at the IPO price. Part of the deal was contingent upon the continued employment of Rob Malda and Jeff Bates and on "the achievement of certain milestones". With the acquisition of Slashdot, Andover.net could now advertise itself as "the leading Linux/Open Source destination on the Internet".[] [] Andover.net eventually merged with VA Linux on February 3, 2000,[] which changed its name to SourceForge, Inc. on May 24, 2007, and became Geeknet, Inc. on November 4, 2009.[]

Slashdot's 10,000th article was posted after two and a half years on February 24, 2000,[] and the 100,000th article was posted on December 11, 2009 after 12 years online.[] During the first 12 years, the most active story with the most responses posted was the post-2004 US Presidential Election article "Kerry Concedes Election To Bush" with 5,687 posts. This followed the creation of a new article section, *politics.slashdot.org*, created at the start of the 2004 election on September 7, 2004.[] Many of the most popular stories are political, with "Strike on Iraq" (March 19, 2003) the second-most-active article and "Barack Obama Wins US Presidency" (November 5, 2008) the third-most-active. The rest of the 10 most active articles are an article announcing the 2005 London bombings, and several articles about Evolution vs. Intelligent Design, Saddam Hussein's capture, and *Fahrenheit 9/11*. Articles about Microsoft and its Windows Operating System are popular—a thread posted in 2002 titled "What's Keeping

You On Windows?" was the 10th-most-active story, and an article about Windows 2000/NT4 source-code leaks the most visited article with more than 680,000 hits.[]

Some controversy erupted on March 9, 2001 after an anonymous user posted the full text of Scientology's "Operating Thetan Level Three" (OT III) document in a comment attached to a Slashdot article. The Church of Scientology demanded that Slashdot remove the document under the Digital Millennium Copyright Act. A week later, in a long article, Slashdot editors explained their decision to remove the page while providing links and information on how to get the document from other sources.[]

Slashdot Japan was launched on May 28, 2001 (although the first article was published April 5, 2001) and is an official offshoot of the US-based Web site. The site is currently owned by OSDN-Japan, Inc., and carries some of the US-based Slashdot articles as well as localized stories.[] [] An external site, *todhsalS*, has reported selected stories published on Slashdot Japan in English since March 1, 2009.[]

On Valentine's Day 2002, founder Rob Malda proposed to longtime girlfriend Kathleen Fent using the front page of Slashdot.[] [] They were married on December 8, 2002, in Las Vegas, Nevada.[]

Slashdot implemented a subscription service on March 1, 2002. Slashdot's subscription model works by allowing users to pay a small fee to be able to view pages without banner ads, starting at a rate of $5 per 1,000 page views – non-subscribers may still view articles and respond to comments, with banner ads in place.[] On March 6, 2003, subscribers were given the ability to see articles 10 to 20 minutes before they are released to the public.[]

Slashdot altered its threaded discussion forum display software to explicitly show domains for links in articles, as "users made a sport out of tricking unsuspecting readers into visiting [Goatse.cx]."[]

April Fools' Day 2006 logo

In observance of April Fools' Day (April 1) in 2006, Slashdot temporarily changed its signature teal color theme to a warm palette of bubblegum pink and changed its masthead from the usual, "News for Nerds" motto to, "OMG!!! Ponies!!!" Editors joked that this was done to increase female readership.[] In another supposed April Fools' Day joke, User Achievement tags were introduced on April 1, 2009.[] This system allowed users to be tagged with various achievements, such as "The Tagger" for tagging a story or "Member of the {1,2,3,4,5} Digit UID Club" for having a Slashdot UID consisting of a certain number of digits. While it was posted on April Fools' Day to allow for certain joke achievements, the system is real.[]

Slashdot unveiled its newly redesigned site on June 4, 2006, following a CSS Redesign Competition. The winner of the competition was Alex Bendiken, who built on the initial CSS framework of the site. The new site looks similar to the old one but is more polished with more rounded curves, collapsible menus, and updated fonts.[] On November 9 that same year, Malda wrote that Slashdot attained 16,777,215 (or $2^{24} - 1$) comments, which broke the database for three hours until the administrators fixed the issue.[]

On January 25, 2011, Malda announced that the site launched its third major redesign in its 13.5-year history, which gutted the HTML and CSS, and updated the graphics.[]

On August 25, 2011, Malda announced that he was resigning as Editor-in-Chief of Slashdot, effective immediately. He did not mention any immediate plans for the future, other than spending more time with his family, catching up on some reading, and possibly writing a book.[] [] His final farewell message received over 1,400 posts within 24 hours on the site.[]

On December 7, 2011, Slashdot announced that it would start to push what the company described as "sponsored" Ask Slashdot questions.[2]

On March 28, 2012, Slashdot announced the launch of slashdot TV.[3]

In September 2012, it was announced that Slashdot had been acquired by Dice Holdings, alongside other Geeknet websites including SourceForge and Freecode, for $20 million in cash.[1] [4] Dice, owner of job listing and career websites, stated that there were no plans for major changes to Slashdot.[4]

Administration

Team

Rob Malda, Founder of Slashdot

The site is owned by Dice Holdings. It was run by its founder, Rob "CmdrTaco" Malda, from 1998 until 2011. He shared editorial responsibilities with several other editors including Timothy Lord, Patrick "Scuttlemonkey" McGarry, Jeff "Soulskill" Boehm, Rob "Samzenpus" Rozeboom, and Keith Dawson.[] [] Jonathan "cowboyneal" Pater is another popular editor of Slashdot, who came to work for Slashdot as a programmer and systems administrator. His online nickname (handle), CowboyNeal, is inspired by a Grateful Dead tribute to Neal Cassady in their song, *"That's It for the Other One"*. He is best known as the target of the usual comic poll option,[] a tradition started by Chris DiBona.[5]

Slash and peer moderation

The administration of the site uses the Slash source code and database, a content management system available under the GNU General Public License.[] Slashdot's editors are primarily responsible for selecting and editing the primary stories daily from submitters like Roland Piquepaille; they provide a one-paragraph summary for each and a link to an external site where the story originated. Each story becomes the topic for a threaded discussion among the site's users.[] A user-based moderation system is employed to filter out abusive comments.[] Every comment is initially given a score of *-1* to *+2*, with a default score of *+1* for registered users, *0* for anonymous users (Anonymous Coward), *+2* for users with high "karma", or *−1* for users with low "karma". As moderators read comments attached to articles, they click to moderate the comment, either up (*+1*) or down (*−1*). Moderators may choose to attach a particular descriptor to the comments as well, such as *normal*, *offtopic*, *flamebait*, *troll*, *redundant*, *insightful*, *interesting*, *informative*, *funny*, *overrated*, or *underrated*, with each corresponding to a *-1* or *+1* rating. So a comment may be seen to have a rating of "+1 insightful" or "-1 troll".[]

Moderation points add to a user's karma, and users with high "karma" are eligible to become moderators themselves. The system does not promote regular users as "moderators" and instead assigns five moderation points at a time to users based on the number of comments they have entered in the system – once a user's moderation points are used up, they can no longer moderate articles (though they can be assigned more moderation points at a later date). Paid staff editors have an unlimited number of moderation points.[] [] []

A given comment can have any integer score from *-1* to *+5*, and registered users of Slashdot can set a personal threshold so that no comments with a lesser score are displayed.[] [] For instance, a user reading Slashdot at level *+5* will only see the highest rated comments, while a user reading at level *-1* will see a more "unfiltered, anarchic version".[]

A meta-moderation system was implemented on September 7, 1999,[] to moderate the moderators and help contain abuses in the moderation system. Meta-moderators are presented with a set of moderations that they may rate as either *fair* or *unfair*. For each moderation, the meta-moderator sees the original comment and the reason assigned by the moderator (e.g. *troll*, *funny*), and the meta-moderator can click to see the context of comments surrounding the one that was moderated.[] []

Features

Slashdot features discussion forums on a variety of technology- and science-related topics, or "News for Nerds", as its motto states. The site is well known for its bias towards the open source software movement.[] Articles are divided into the following sections:[]

- *Apple* – news related to products from Apple Inc., such as Mac OS X or iPhone.
- *Ask Slashdot* – articles that seek advice from users about jobs, computer hardware, software glitches, philosophical problems, or more.
- *Book Reviews* – original book reviews on (not necessarily) tech books.
- *BSD* – news about the various modern versions of UNIX derived from the UCB distribution.
- *Developers* – news about software or programming.
- *Features* – original, feature-length articles.
- *Games* – gaming news.
- *Geeks in Space* – a web audio broadcast featuring several of the editors of Slashdot (outdated; no new episodes have been posted recently).
- *Idle* – miscellaneous and humorous articles, pictures, and videos.
- *Interviews* – interviews with various people related to science and technology.
- *Information Technology* (IT) – anything that people with "Information Technology" in their job description might be interested to know.
- *Linux* – news specific to the Linux operating system (any variant or distribution).
- *Politics* – news typically relevant to politics of the United States, but occasionally featuring international political news. It was originally created to cover the 2004 United States Presidential Election.
- *Polls* – a poll is usually run on the site in the right-hand margin, asking users their choice on a variety of topics. In the earlier years of the site, one of the options that could be selected was *CowboyNeal*, the handle of Jonathan Pater, an administrator of the site. This became known as the *CowboyNeal option*.[] During the summer of 2005, he stopped being in charge of the polls, and as a result the *CowboyNeal option* all but disappeared.
- *Science* – news on science-related topics (e.g. cool technology, space telescope observations, interesting medical research).
- *Your Rights Online* (YRO) – news on topics pertaining to internet privacy and digital rights.

Tags

Slashdot uses a system of "tags" where users can categorize a story to group them together and sorting them. Tags are written in all lowercase, with no spaces, and limited to 64 characters. For example, articles could be tagged as being about *security* or *mozilla*. Some articles are tagged with longer tags, such as *whatcouldpossiblygowrong* (expressing the perception of catastrophic risk), *suddenoutbreakofcommonsense* (used when the community feels that the subject has finally figured out something obvious), *correlationnotcausation* (used when scientific articles lack direct evidence; see correlation does not imply causation), or *getyourasstomars* (commonly seen in articles about Mars or space exploration).[] [6]

Culture

Tux, the Linux Penguin

As an online community with primarily user-generated content, many in-jokes and internet memes have developed over the course of the site's history. A popular meme (based on an unscientific Slashdot user poll[7]) is, "In Soviet Russia, *noun verb* you!"[8] The phrase was actually originated by Ukrainian-born comedian Yakov Smirnoff as his famous Russian reversal – "In America, you can always find a party. In Soviet Russia, The Party can always find you!"[] Other popular memes usually pertain to computing or technology, such as "Imagine a Beowulf cluster of these",[] "But does it run Linux?",[] or "Netcraft now confirms: BSD (or some other software package or item) is dying."[] Some users will also refer to seemingly innocent remarks by correcting them and adding "you insensitive clod!" to the statement – a reference to a February 14, 1986, *Calvin & Hobbes* cartoon[] or the 11th season *The Simpsons* episode, *Last Tap Dance in Springfield*, wherein Frink exclaims to Homer, "I was merely trying to spare the girl's feelings, you insensitive clod!" Users will also typically refer to articles referring to data storage and data capacity by inquiring how much it is in units of Libraries of Congress.[]

Slashdotters often use the abbreviation TFA which stands for *The fucking article* or RTFA (*Read the fucking article*), which itself is derived from the abbreviation RTFM.[] Usage of this abbreviation often exposes comments from posters who have not read the article linked to in the main story.

Slashdotters typically like to mock United States Senator Ted Stevens' 2006 description of the Internet as a "series of tubes"[] [] or Microsoft CEO Steve Ballmer's chair-throwing incident from 2005.[] [] Microsoft founder Bill Gates is a popular target of jokes by Slashdotters, and all stories about Microsoft were once identified with a graphic of Gates looking like a Borg from *Star Trek: The Next Generation*.[] Many Slashdotters have long talked about the supposed release of *Duke Nukem Forever*, which was promised in 1997 but was delayed indefinitely (the game was eventually released in 2011).[] References to the game are commonly brought up in other articles about software packages that are not yet in production even though the announced delivery date has long passed (see vaporware).

Having a low Slashdot user identifier (user ID) is highly valued since they are assigned sequentially; having one is a sign that someone has an older account and has contributed to the site longer. For Slashdot's 10-year anniversary in 2007, one of the items auctioned off in the charity auction for the Electronic Frontier Foundation was a 3-digit Slashdot user ID.[] []

Traffic and publicity

As of 2006, Slashdot had approximately 5.5 million users per month. As of January 2013, the site's Alexa rank is 2,000, with the average user spending 3 minutes and 18 seconds per day on the site and 82,665 sites linking in.[] The primary stories on the site consist of a short synopsis paragraph, a link to the original story, and a lengthy discussion section, all contributed by users. Discussion on stories can get up to 10,000 posts per day. Slashdot has been considered a pioneer in user-driven content, influencing other sites such as Google News and Wikipedia.[] [] However, there has been a dip in readership as of 2011, primarily due to the increase of technology-related blogs and Twitter feeds.[] In 2002, approximately 50% of Slashdot's traffic consisted of people who simply check out the headlines and click through, while others participate in discussion boards and take part in the community.[] Many links in Slashdot stories caused the linked site to get swamped by heavy traffic and its server to collapse. This is known as the "Slashdot effect",[] [] a term which was first coined on February 15, 1999 that refers to an article about a "new generation of niche Web portals driving unprecedented amounts of traffic to sites of interest".[] [] Today, most major websites can handle the surge of traffic, but the effect continues to occur on smaller or independent sites.[] These sites are then said to have been *Slashdotted*.

Slashdot has received over twenty awards, including People's Voice Awards in 2000 in both of the categories for which it was nominated (*Best Community Site* and *Best News Site*).[] It was also voted as one of *Newsweek*'s favorite technology Web sites and rated in Yahoo!'s Top 100 Web sites as the "Best Geek Hangout" (2001).[] The main antagonists in the 2004 novel *Century Rain*, by Alastair Reynolds – The Slashers – are named after Slashdot users.[] The site was mentioned briefly in the 2000 novel *Cosmonaut Keep*, written by Ken MacLeod.[] Several celebrities have stated that they either checked the website regularly or participated in its discussion forums using an account. Some of these celebrities include: Apple co-founder Steve Wozniak,[] writer and actor Wil Wheaton,[] and id Software technical director John Carmack.[]

See also

- Digg
- Fark
- Reddit

References

[1] http://www.diceholdingsinc.com/phoenix.zhtml?c=211152&p=irol-newsArticle&ID=1735911
[4] http://www.h-online.com/open/news/item/Dice-Holdings-acquires-Slashdot-and-SourceForge-1711181.html
[8] As an example, the phrase "You use the computer" would translate into "In Soviet Russia, the computer uses you!"

External links

- Slashdot (http://slashdot.org/) (Mobile (http://m.slashdot.org))
- Slashdot Japan (http://slashdot.jp/)
- A Brief History of Slashdot:
  - Part 1, Chips & Dips (http://meta.slashdot.org/article.pl?sid=07/10/02/1553218)
  - Part 2, Explosions (http://meta.slashdot.org/article.pl?sid=07/10/10/1445216)
  - Part 3, Going Corporate (http://meta.slashdot.org/article.pl?sid=07/10/17/1412245)
  - Part 4, Yesterday, Today, Tomorrow (http://meta.slashdot.org/article.pl?sid=07/10/31/1631213)

Denial-of-service_attack

In computing, a **denial-of-service attack (DoS attack)** or **distributed denial-of-service attack (DDoS attack)** is an attempt to make a machine or network resource unavailable to its intended users. Although the means to carry out, motives for, and targets of a DoS attack may vary, it generally consists of efforts to temporarily or indefinitely interrupt or suspend services of a host connected to the Internet.

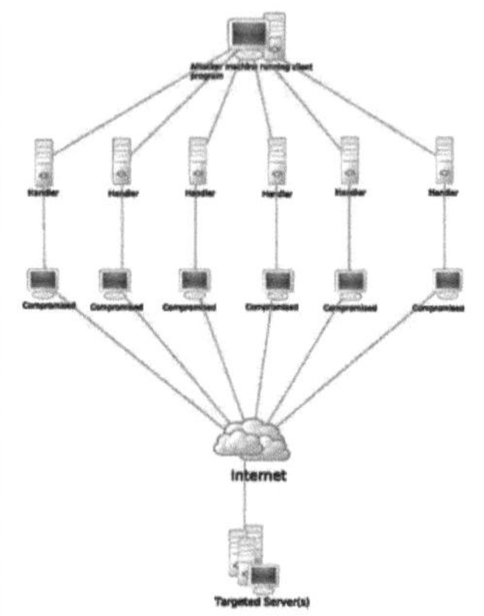

DDoS Stacheldraht Attack diagram.

Perpetrators of DoS attacks typically target sites or services hosted on high-profile web servers such as banks, credit card payment gateways, and even root nameservers. This technique has now seen extensive use in certain games, used by server owners, or disgruntled competitors on games. Increasingly, DoS attacks have also been used as a form of resistance. DoS they say is a tool for registering dissent. Richard Stallman has stated that DoS is a form of 'Internet Street Protests'.[1] The term is generally used relating to computer networks, but is not limited to this field; for example, it is also used in reference to CPU resource management.[2]

One common method of attack involves saturating the target machine with external communications requests, so much so that it cannot respond to legitimate traffic, or responds so slowly as to be rendered essentially unavailable. Such attacks usually lead to a server overload. In general terms, DoS attacks are implemented by either forcing the targeted computer(s) to reset, or consuming its resources so that it can no longer provide its intended service or obstructing the communication media between the intended users and the victim so that they can no longer communicate adequately.

Denial-of-service attacks are considered violations of the Internet Architecture Board's Internet proper use policy, and also violate the acceptable use policies of virtually all Internet service providers. They also commonly constitute violations of the laws of individual nations.

Symptoms and manifestations

The United States Computer Emergency Readiness Team (US-CERT) defines symptoms of denial-of-service attacks to include:

- Unusually slow network performance (opening files or accessing web sites)
- Unavailability of a particular web site
- Inability to access any web site
- Dramatic increase in the number of spam emails received—(this type of DoS attack is considered an e-mail bomb)[]
- Disconnection of a wireless or wired internet connection

Denial-of-service attacks can also lead to problems in the network 'branches' around the actual computer being attacked. For example, the bandwidth of a router between the Internet and a LAN may be consumed by an attack, compromising not only the intended computer, but also the entire network or other computers on the LAN.[3]

If the attack is conducted on a sufficiently large scale, entire geographical regions of Internet connectivity can be compromised without the attacker's knowledge or intent by incorrectly configured or flimsy network infrastructure equipment.

Methods of attack

A denial-of-service attack is characterized by an explicit attempt by attackers to prevent legitimate users of a service from using that service. There are two general forms of DoS attacks: those that crash services and those that flood services.

A DoS attack can be perpetrated in a number of ways. The five basic types of attack are:

1. Consumption of computational resources, such as bandwidth, disk space, or processor time.
2. Disruption of configuration information, such as routing information.
3. Disruption of state information, such as unsolicited resetting of TCP sessions.
4. Disruption of physical network components.
5. Obstructing the communication media between the intended users and the victim so that they can no longer communicate adequately.

A DoS attack may include execution of malware intended to:

- Max out the processor's usage, preventing any work from occurring.
- Trigger errors in the microcode of the machine.
- Trigger errors in the sequencing of instructions, so as to force the computer into an unstable state or lock-up.
- Exploit errors in the operating system, causing resource starvation and/or thrashing, i.e. to use up all available facilities so no real work can be accomplished or it can crash the system itself
- Crash the operating system itself.

In most cases DoS attacks involve forging of IP sender addresses (IP address spoofing) so that the location of the attacking machines cannot easily be identified and to prevent filtering of the packets based on the source address.

Internet Control Message Protocol (ICMP) flood

A smurf attack is one particular variant of a flooding DoS attack on the public Internet. It relies on misconfigured network devices that allow packets to be sent to all computer hosts on a particular network via the broadcast address of the network, rather than a specific machine. The network then serves as a smurf amplifier. In such an attack, the perpetrators will send large numbers of IP packets with the source address faked to appear to be the address of the victim. The network's bandwidth is quickly used up, preventing legitimate packets from getting through to their destination.[] To combat denial of service attacks on the Internet, services like the Smurf Amplifier Registry have given network service providers the ability to identify misconfigured networks and to take appropriate action such as filtering.

Ping flood is based on sending the victim an overwhelming number of ping packets, usually using the "ping" command from Unix-like hosts (the -t flag on Windows systems is much less capable of overwhelming a target, also the -l (size) flag does not allow sent packet size greater than 65500 in Windows). It is very simple to launch, the primary requirement being access to greater bandwidth than the victim.

Ping of death is based on sending the victim a malformed ping packet, which might lead to a system crash.

(S)SYN flood

A SYN flood occurs when a host sends a flood of TCP/SYN packets, often with a forged sender address. Each of these packets is handled like a connection request, causing the server to spawn a half-open connection, by sending back a TCP/SYN-ACK packet (Acknowledge), and waiting for a packet in response from the sender address (response to the ACK Packet). However, because the sender address is forged, the response never comes. These half-open connections saturate the number of available connections the server is able to make, keeping it from responding to legitimate requests until after the attack ends.[4]

Teardrop attacks

A teardrop attack involves sending mangled IP fragments with overlapping, over-sized payloads to the target machine. This can crash various operating systems because of a bug in their TCP/IP fragmentation re-assembly code.[] Windows 3.1x, Windows 95 and Windows NT operating systems, as well as versions of Linux prior to versions 2.0.32 and 2.1.63 are vulnerable to this attack.

Around September 2009, a vulnerability in Windows Vista was referred to as a "teardrop attack", but the attack targeted SMB2 which is a higher layer than the TCP packets that teardrop used.[5] [6]

Low-rate Denial-of-Service attacks

The Low-rate DoS (LDoS) attack exploits TCP's slow-time-scale dynamics of retransmission time-out (RTO) mechanisms to reduce TCP throughput. Basically, an attacker can cause a TCP flow to repeatedly enter a RTO state by sending high-rate, but short-duration bursts, and repeating periodically at slower RTO time-scales. The TCP throughput at the attacked node will be significantly reduced while the attacker will have low average rate making it difficult to be detected.[7]

Peer-to-peer attacks

Attackers have found a way to exploit a number of bugs in peer-to-peer servers to initiate DDoS attacks. The most aggressive of these peer-to-peer-DDoS attacks exploits DC++. Peer-to-peer attacks are different from regular botnet-based attacks. With peer-to-peer there is no botnet and the attacker does not have to communicate with the clients it subverts. Instead, the attacker acts as a "puppet master," instructing clients of large peer-to-peer file sharing hubs to disconnect from their peer-to-peer network and to connect to the victim's website instead. As a result, several thousand computers may aggressively try to connect to a target website. While a typical web server can handle a few hundred connections per second before performance begins to degrade, most web servers fail almost instantly under five or six thousand connections per second. With a moderately large peer-to-peer attack, a site could potentially be hit with up to 750,000 connections in short order. The targeted web server will be plugged up by the incoming connections.

While peer-to-peer attacks are easy to identify with signatures, the large number of IP addresses that need to be blocked (often over 250,000 during the course of a large-scale attack) means that this type of attack can overwhelm mitigation defenses. Even if a mitigation device can keep blocking IP addresses, there are other problems to consider. For instance, there is a brief moment where the connection is opened on the server side before the signature itself comes through. Only once the connection is opened to the server can the identifying signature be sent and detected, and the connection torn down. Even tearing down connections takes server resources and can harm the server.

This method of attack can be prevented by specifying in the peer-to-peer protocol which ports are allowed or not. If port 80 is not allowed, the possibilities for attack on websites can be very limited.

Asymmetry of resource utilization in starvation attacks

An attack which is successful in consuming resources on the victim computer must be either:

- carried out by an attacker with greater resources, by either:
  - controlling a computer with greater computation power or, more commonly, large network bandwidth
  - controlling a large number of computers and directing them to attack as a group. A DDoS attack is the primary example of this.
- taking advantage of a property of the operating system or applications on the victim system which enables an attack consuming vastly more of the victim's resources than the attacker's (an asymmetric attack). Smurf attack, SYN flood, Sockstress and NAPTHA attack are all asymmetric attacks.

An attack may utilize a combination of these methods in order to magnify its power.

Permanent denial-of-service attacks

A permanent denial-of-service (PDoS), also known loosely as phlashing,[8] is an attack that damages a system so badly that it requires replacement or reinstallation of hardware.[] Unlike the distributed denial-of-service attack, a PDoS attack exploits security flaws which allow remote administration on the management interfaces of the victim's hardware, such as routers, printers, or other networking hardware. The attacker uses these vulnerabilities to replace a device's firmware with a modified, corrupt, or defective firmware image—a process which when done legitimately is known as *flashing*. This therefore "bricks" the device, rendering it unusable for its original purpose until it can be repaired or replaced.

The PDoS is a pure hardware targeted attack which can be much faster and requires fewer resources than using a botnet in a DDoS attack. Because of these features, and the potential and high probability of security exploits on Network Enabled Embedded Devices (NEEDs), this technique has come to the attention of numerous hacker communities.

PhlashDance is a tool created by Rich Smith (an employee of Hewlett-Packard's Systems Security Lab) used to detect and demonstrate PDoS vulnerabilities at the 2008 EUSecWest Applied Security Conference [9] in London.[]

Application-level floods

Various DoS-causing exploits such as buffer overflow can cause server-running software to get confused and fill the disk space or consume all available memory or CPU time.

Other kinds of DoS rely primarily on brute force, flooding the target with an overwhelming flux of packets, oversaturating its connection bandwidth or depleting the target's system resources. Bandwidth-saturating floods rely on the attacker having higher bandwidth available than the victim; a common way of achieving this today is via Distributed Denial of Service, employing a botnet. Other floods may use specific packet types or connection requests to saturate finite resources by, for example, occupying the maximum number of open connections or filling the victim's disk space with logs.

A "banana attack" is another particular type of DoS. It involves redirecting outgoing messages from the client back onto the client, preventing outside access, as well as flooding the client with the sent packets.

An attacker with shell-level access to a victim's computer may slow it until it is unusable or crash it by using a fork bomb.

A kind of application-level DoS attack is XDoS (or XML DoS) which can be controlled by modern Web Application Firewalls (WAFs).

Nuke

A Nuke is an old denial-of-service attack against computer networks consisting of fragmented or otherwise invalid ICMP packets sent to the target, achieved by using a modified ping utility to repeatedly send this corrupt data, thus slowing down the affected computer until it comes to a complete stop.

A specific example of a nuke attack that gained some prominence is the WinNuke, which exploited the vulnerability in the NetBIOS handler in Windows 95. A string of out-of-band data was sent to TCP port 139 of the victim's machine, causing it to lock up and display a Blue Screen of Death (BSOD).

OWASP HTTP Post Denial of Service Tool

From the authority of web application security OWASP Foundation [10] the OWASP HTTP Post Tool [11] completes the request headers phase however it sends the request body (post payload) very slowly (e.g. - 1 byte/110sec). When you consider that, by default, Apache will accept a request body of up to 2GB in size, you can can see how effective this attack can be.

R-U-Dead-Yet? (RUDY)

This attack is one of many web application DoS tools available to directly attack web applications by starvation of available sessions on the web server. Much like Slowloris, RUDY keeps sessions at halt using never-ending POST transmissions and sending an arbitrarily large content-length header value.

Slow Read attack

Slow Read attack sends legitimate application layer requests but reads responses very slowly, thus trying to exhaust the server's connection pool. Slow reading is achieved by advertising very small number for the TCP Receive Window size and at the same time by emptying clients' TCP receive buffer slowly. That naturally ensures a very low data flow rate.

Distributed attack

A distributed denial of service attack (DDoS) occurs when multiple systems flood the bandwidth or resources of a targeted system, usually one or more web servers. This is the result of multiple compromised systems (for example a botnet) flooding the targeted system(s) with traffic. When a server is overloaded with connections, new connections can no longer be accepted.

Malware can carry DDoS attack mechanisms; one of the better-known examples of this was MyDoom. Its DoS mechanism was triggered on a specific date and time. This type of DDoS involved hardcoding the target IP address prior to release of the malware and no further interaction was necessary to launch the attack.

A system may also be compromised with a trojan, allowing the attacker to download a zombie agent (or the trojan may contain one). Attackers can also break into systems using automated tools that exploit flaws in programs that listen for connections from remote hosts. This scenario primarily concerns systems acting as servers on the web.

Stacheldraht is a classic example of a DDoS tool. It utilizes a layered structure where the attacker uses a client program to connect to handlers, which are compromised systems that issue commands to the zombie agents, which in turn facilitate the DDoS attack. Agents are compromised via the handlers by the attacker, using automated routines to exploit vulnerabilities in programs that accept remote connections running on the targeted remote hosts. Each handler can control up to a thousand agents.[12]

These collections of systems compromisers are known as botnets. DDoS tools like Stacheldraht still use classic DoS attack methods centered on IP spoofing and amplification like smurf attacks and fraggle attacks (these are also known as bandwidth consumption attacks). SYN floods (also known as resource starvation attacks) may also be used. Newer tools can use DNS servers for DoS purposes. See next section.

Simple attacks such as SYN floods may appear with a wide range of source IP addresses, giving the appearance of a well distributed DoS. These flood attacks do not require completion of the TCP three way handshake and attempt to exhaust the destination SYN queue or the server bandwidth. Because the source IP addresses can be trivially spoofed, an attack could come from a limited set of sources, or may even originate from a single host. Stack enhancements such as syn cookies may be effective mitigation against SYN queue flooding, however complete bandwidth exhaustion may require involvement.

Unlike MyDoom's DDoS mechanism, botnets can be turned against any IP address. Script kiddies use them to deny the availability of well known websites to legitimate users.[] More sophisticated attackers use DDoS tools for the purposes of extortion – even against their business rivals.[13]

If an attacker mounts an attack from a single host it would be classified as a DoS attack. In fact, any attack against availability would be classed as a Denial of Service attack. On the other hand, if an attacker uses many systems to simultaneously launch attacks against a remote host, this would be classified as a DDoS attack.

The major advantages to an attacker of using a distributed denial-of-service attack are that: multiple machines can generate more attack traffic than one machine, multiple attack machines are harder to turn off than one attack machine, and that the behavior of each attack machine can be stealthier, making it harder to track and shut down. These attacker advantages cause challenges for defense mechanisms. For example, merely purchasing more incoming bandwidth than the current volume of the attack might not help, because the attacker might be able to simply add more attack machines.

In some cases a machine may become part of a DDoS attack with the owner's consent, for example, in Operation Payback, organized by the group Anonymous.

Reflected / Spoofed attack

A distributed reflected denial of service attack (DRDoS) involves sending forged requests of some type to a very large number of computers that will reply to the requests. Using Internet Protocol address spoofing, the source address is set to that of the targeted victim, which means all the replies will go to (and flood) the target.

ICMP Echo Request attacks (Smurf Attack) can be considered one form of reflected attack, as the flooding host(s) send Echo Requests to the broadcast addresses of mis-configured networks, thereby enticing many hosts to send Echo Reply packets to the victim. Some early DDoS programs implemented a distributed form of this attack.

Many services can be exploited to act as reflectors, some harder to block than others.[14] DNS amplification attacks involve a new mechanism that increased the amplification effect, using a much larger list of DNS servers than seen earlier.[15] [16]

Telephony denial of service

Voice over IP has made abusive origination of large numbers of telephone voice calls inexpensive and readily automatised while permitting call origins to be misrepresented through caller ID spoofing.

According to the US Federal Bureau of Investigation, TDoS has appeared as part of various fraudulent schemes:

- A scammer contacts the victim's banker or broker, impersonating the victim to request a funds transfer. The banker's attempt to contact the victim for verification of the transfer fails as the victim's telephone lines are being flooded with thousands of bogus calls, rendering the victim unreachable.[17]
- A scammer contacts consumers with a bogus claim to collect an outstanding payday loan for thousands of dollars. When the consumer objects, the scammer retaliates by flooding the victim's employer with thousands of automated calls. In some cases, displayed caller ID is spoofed to impersonate police or law enforcement agencies.[18]
- A scammer contacts consumers with a bogus debt collection demand and threatens to send police; when the victim balks, the scammer floods local police numbers with calls on which caller ID is spoofed to display the victims number. Police soon arrive at the victim's residence attempting to find the origin of the calls.

Telephony denial of service can exist even without Internet telephony. In the 2002 New Hampshire Senate election phone jamming scandal, telemarketers were used to flood political opponents with spurious calls to jam phone banks on election day. Widespread publication of a number can also flood it with enough calls to render it unusable, as happened with multiple +1-area code-867-5309 subscribers inundated by hundreds of misdialed calls daily in response to a popular song 867-5309/Jenny.

TDoS differs from other telephone harassment (such as prank calls and obscene phone calls) by the number of calls originated; by occupying lines continuously with repeated automated calls, the victim is prevented from making or receiving both routine and emergency telephone calls.

Related exploits include SMS flooding attacks and black fax or fax loop transmission.

Unintentional denial of service

This describes a situation where a website ends up denied, not due to a deliberate attack by a single individual or group of individuals, but simply due to a sudden enormous spike in popularity. This can happen when an extremely popular website posts a prominent link to a second, less well-prepared site, for example, as part of a news story. The result is that a significant proportion of the primary site's regular users – potentially hundreds of thousands of people – click that link in the space of a few hours, having the same effect on the target website as a DDoS attack. A VIPDoS is the same, but specifically when the link was posted by a celebrity.

When Michael Jackson died in 2009, websites such as Google and Twitter slowed down or even crashed.[19] Many sites' servers thought the requests were from a virus or spyware trying to cause a Denial of Service attack, warning users that their queries looked like "automated requests from a computer virus or spyware application".[20]

News sites and link sites – sites whose primary function is to provide links to interesting content elsewhere on the Internet – are most likely to cause this phenomenon. The canonical example is the Slashdot effect when receiving traffic from Slashdot. Sites such as Reddit, Digg, the Drudge Report, Fark, Something Awful, and the webcomic Penny Arcade have their own corresponding "effects", known as "DDoS of Love", "the Digg effect", being "drudged", "farking", "goonrushing" and "wanging"; respectively.

Routers have also been known to create unintentional DoS attacks, as both D-Link and Netgear routers have created NTP vandalism by flooding NTP servers without respecting the restrictions of client types or geographical limitations.

Similar unintentional denials of service can also occur via other media, e.g. when a URL is mentioned on television. If a server is being indexed by Google or another search engine during peak periods of activity, or does not have a lot of available bandwidth while being indexed, it can also experience the effects of a DoS attack.

Legal action has been taken in at least one such case. In 2006, Universal Tube & Rollform Equipment Corporation sued YouTube: massive numbers of would-be youtube.com users accidentally typed the tube company's URL, utube.com. As a result, the tube company ended up having to spend large amounts of money on upgrading their bandwidth.[21]

Denial-of-Service Level II

The goal of DoS L2 (possibly DDoS) attack is to cause a launching of a defense mechanism which blocks the network segment from which the attack originated. In case of distributed attack or IP header modification (that depends on the kind of security behavior) it will fully block the attacked network from Internet, but without system crash.

Performing DoS-attacks

A wide array of programs are used to launch DoS-attacks. Most of these programs are completely focused on performing DoS-attacks, while others are also true Packet injectors, thus able to perform other tasks as well. Such tools are intended for benign use, but they can also be utilized in launching attacks on victim networks.

Handling

Defensive responses to Denial of Service attacks typically involves the use of a combination of attack detection, traffic classification and response tools, aiming to block traffic that they identify as illegitimate and allow traffic that they identify as legitimate.[22] A list of prevention and response tools is provided below:

Firewalls

Firewalls can be set up to have simple rules such to allow or deny protocols, ports or IP addresses. In the case of a simple attack coming from a small number of unusual IP addresses for instance, one could put up a simple rule to drop all incoming traffic from those attackers.

More complex attacks will however be hard to block with simple rules: for example, if there is an ongoing attack on port 80 (web service), it is not possible to drop all incoming traffic on this port because doing so will prevent the server from serving legitimate traffic.[23] Additionally, firewalls may be too deep in the network hierarchy. Routers may be affected before the traffic gets to the firewall. Nonetheless, firewalls can effectively prevent users from launching simple flooding type attacks from machines behind the firewall.

Some stateful firewalls, like OpenBSD's pf(4) packet filter, can act as a proxy for connections: the handshake is validated (with the client) instead of simply forwarding the packet to the destination. It is available for other BSDs as well. In that context, it is called "synproxy".

Switches

Most switches have some rate-limiting and ACL capability. Some switches provide automatic and/or system-wide rate limiting, traffic shaping, delayed binding (TCP splicing), deep packet inspection and Bogon filtering (bogus IP filtering) to detect and remediate denial of service attacks through automatic rate filtering and WAN Link failover and balancing.

These schemes will work as long as the DoS attacks are something that can be prevented by using them. For example SYN flood can be prevented using delayed binding or TCP splicing. Similarly content based DoS may be prevented using deep packet inspection. Attacks originating from dark addresses or going to dark addresses can be prevented using Bogon filtering. Automatic rate filtering can work as long as you have set rate-thresholds correctly and granularly. Wan-link failover will work as long as both links have DoS/DDoS prevention mechanism.

Routers

Similar to switches, routers have some rate-limiting and ACL capability. They, too, are manually set. Most routers can be easily overwhelmed under a DoS attack. Cisco IOS has features that prevent flooding, i.e. example settings.[24]

Application front end hardware

Application front end hardware is intelligent hardware placed on the network before traffic reaches the servers. It can be used on networks in conjunction with routers and switches. Application front end hardware analyzes data packets as they enter the system, and then identifies them as priority, regular, or dangerous. There are more than 25 bandwidth management vendors.

IPS based prevention

Intrusion-prevention systems (IPS) are effective if the attacks have signatures associated with them. However, the trend among the attacks is to have legitimate content but bad intent. Intrusion-prevention systems which work on content recognition cannot block behavior-based DoS attacks.

An ASIC based IPS may detect and block denial of service attacks because they have the processing power and the granularity to analyze the attacks and act like a circuit breaker in an automated way.

A rate-based IPS (RBIPS) must analyze traffic granularly and continuously monitor the traffic pattern and determine if there is traffic anomaly. It must let the legitimate traffic flow while blocking the DoS attack traffic. [25]

DDS based defense

More focused on the problem than IPS, a DoS Defense System (DDS) is able to block connection-based DoS attacks and those with legitimate content but bad intent. A DDS can also address both protocol attacks (such as Teardrop and Ping of death) and rate-based attacks (such as ICMP floods and SYN floods).

Blackholing and sinkholing

With blackholing, all the traffic to the attacked DNS or IP address is sent to a "black hole" (null interface or a non-existent server). To be more efficient and avoid affecting network connectivity, it can be managed by the ISP.[26]

Sinkholing routes traffic to a valid IP address which analyzes traffic and rejects bad packets. Sinkholing is not efficient for most severe attacks.

Clean pipes

All traffic is passed through a "cleaning center" or a "scrubbing center" via various methods such as proxies, tunnels or even direct circuits, which separates "bad" traffic (DDoS and also other common internet attacks) and only sends good traffic beyond to the server. The provider needs central connectivity to the Internet to manage this kind of service unless they happen to be located within the same facility as the "cleaning center" or "scrubbing center".[27]

Prolexic, Tata Communications, AT&T and Verisign are examples of providers of this service.[28] [29] [30]

Side effects of DoS attacks

Backscatter

In computer network security, backscatter is a side-effect of a spoofed denial-of-service attack. In this kind of attack, the attacker spoofs (or forges) the source address in IP packets sent to the victim. In general, the victim machine cannot distinguish between the spoofed packets and legitimate packets, so the victim responds to the spoofed packets as it normally would. These response packets are known as backscatter.[31]

If the attacker is spoofing source addresses randomly, the backscatter response packets from the victim will be sent back to random destinations. This effect can be used by network telescopes as indirect evidence of such attacks.

The term "backscatter analysis" refers to observing backscatter packets arriving at a statistically significant portion of the IP address space to determine characteristics of DoS attacks and victims.

Legality

In the Police and Justice Act 2006, the United Kingdom specifically outlawed denial-of-service attacks and set a maximum penalty of 10 years in prison.[32]

In the US, denial-of-service attacks may be considered a federal crime under the Computer Fraud and Abuse Act with penalties that include years of imprisonment. Many other countries have similar laws.[33]

The US situation is under court ruling with a case in California.[34]

On January 7, 2013, Anonymous posted a petition on the whitehouse.gov site asking that DDoS be recognized as a legal form of protest similar to the Occupy protests.[35]

See also

- Billion laughs
- Black fax
- Cybercrime
- Dosnet
- Industrial espionage
- Intrusion-detection system
- LAND
- LOIC
- Network intrusion detection system
- Regular expression Denial of Service
- Slowloris
- Virtual sit-in
- Wireless signal jammer

Notes and references

[1] The Philosophy of Anonymous (http://www.radicalphilosophy.com/article/the-philosophy-of-anonymous)
[2] Error: Bad DOI specified: 10.1109/MSP.2010.2
[7] Error: Bad DOI specified: 10.1109/LCOMM.2010.05.091407
[9] http://eusecwest.com
[10] http://www.owasp.org
[11] https://www.owasp.org/index.php/OWASP_HTTP_Post_Tool
[14] Paxson, Vern (2001), *An Analysis of Using Reflectors for Distributed Denial-of-Service Attacks* (http://www.icir.org/vern/papers/reflectors.CCR.01/reflectors.html)
[15] Vaughn, Randal and Evron, Gadi (2006), *DNS Amplification Attacks* (http://www.isotf.org/news/DNS-Amplification-Attacks.pdf)
[17] http://www.fbi.gov/newark/press-releases/2010/nk051110.htm
[18] http://www.ic3.gov/media/2013/130107.aspx
[22] Error: Bad DOI specified: 10.1093/comjnl/bxp078
[24] "Some IoS tips for Internet Service (Providers)" (http://mehmet.suzen.googlepages.com/qos_ios_dos_suzen2005.pdf) (Mehmet Suzen)
[31] An educational animation describing such backscatter can be found on the animations page (http://www.caida.org/publications/animations/) maintained by the Cooperative Association for Internet Data Analysis.
[32] U.K. outlaws denial-of-service attacks (http://news.cnet.com/U.K.-outlaws-denial-of-service-attacks/2100-7348_3-6134472.html), November 10, 2006, Tom Espiner, CNET News
[34] DDOS Attack: crime or virtual sit-in? (http://www.youtube.com/watch?v=59AlNnX_Ksg&feature=feedu), October 6, 2011, by RT.COM

External links

- RFC 4732 Internet Denial-of-Service Considerations
- Radware Global Security Report (http://www.radware.com/Resources/lp.aspx?campaign=1628918&WT.mc_id=2011) GlobalApplicationNetSecurityReport_HP
- W3C The World Wide Web Security FAQ (http://www.w3.org/Security/Faq/wwwsf6.html)
- Understanding and surviving DDoS attacks (http://www.armoraid.com/survive/)
- cert.org (http://www.cert.org/tech_tips/denial_of_service.html) CERT's Guide to DoS attacks. (historic document)
- ATLAS Summary Report (http://atlas.arbor.net/summary/dos) – Real-time global report of DDoS attacks.
- linuxsecurity.com (http://www.linuxsecurity.com/content/view/121960/49/) An article on preventing DDoS attacks.
- Is Your PC a Zombie? (http://antivirus.about.com/od/whatisavirus/a/zombiepc.htm), About.com.
- Report: Distributed Denial of Service Attacks Against Independent Media and Human Rights Sites (http://cyber.law.harvard.edu/publications/2010/DDoS_Independent_Media_and_Human_Rights) Berkman Center for Internet and Society Report on DDoS
- News on DDoS (http://www.ddosattackprotection.org/) Latest DDoS news and techniques
- Types of DDoS attacks (http://blog.rivalhost.com/12-types-of-ddos-attacks-used-by-hackers/) Various forms of DDoS attacks
- Mitigating Slow HTTP Denial of Service (http://blog.spiderlabs.com/2011/07/advanced-topic-of-the-week-mitigating-slow-http-dos-attacks.html)

Article Sources and Contributors

Allakhazam *Source*: http://en.wikipedia.org/w/index.php?title=Allakhazam *Contributors*: BillWSmithJr, Blake, Danalog, Guyzero, KJS77, Kaelesh, Kariteh, Marluxia.Kyoshu, Martarius, Mdenham, Melsaran, Miracle Pen, Otolemur crassicaudatus, Peter Napkin Party, Phuzion, Pimdip, Polly, Ripvannwinkler, Rjwilmsi, Robofish, RockMFR, Sassythiefx, SharkD, Standingorder, Taelus, Trivialist, 56 anonymous edits

Massively_multiplayer_online_role-playing_game *Source*: http://en.wikipedia.org/w/index.php?title=Massively_multiplayer_online_role-playing_game *Contributors*: 0612, 199, 1ForTheMoney, 20em89.01, 21655, 2602:30B:8211:A2E9:152C:5182:3CF6:4F04, 28421u2232nfenfcenc, 2A02:2F02:FF1:F005:0:0:4F75:A875, 6birc, 7h3 3L173, 95j, A D Monroe III, A J Luxton, A Man In Black, A ghost, A metal shard, AA Pilot16, AAA!, ABunnell, AJR, AS, AUST ZoRrO, AWP Lizard, AaThinker, Aaron Schulz, Aaron Walden, Abelius, AbsolutDan, Abu badali, Accurizer, Aconaway1, Adam Bishop, AdjustShift, Aeon1006, Afluent Rider, Afronomenon, Agateller, Ageekgal, Aitias, Ajshm, Aka042, Akosygin, Al E., Al95521, Alansohn, Alastair, Alderweis, Alex.g, AlexR, Alexzusmo, AllyUnion, Alpdpedia, Amadsen80, Ambarish, Amberrock, Amessora, Amiteli, Anaraug, Andonic, Andquad, Andrew Gray, Andrewpmk, Andy mci, Angel caboodle, AngelHedgie, Angela, AnimeJanai, Anion, Anirluph, Antandrus, Anthony999Thane, AnthonyQBachler, Anturiaethwr, Apparition11, Archetypist, Arda Xi, ArglebargleIV, ArielGold, Arnoox, Arthena, Artisan Codesmith, Ashkenazzi, Aspectacle, Athaenara, AtomicDog1471, Atticon40, Audriusa, Aumakua, Aurasphere, Avillia, AwesomeGuitar22, Axl, AySz88, AzaToth, Aznhan, Azzer007, B3AM, BHC, Barek, Barnacles phd, Barneyboo, Bayz0r, Bcnerfwars, Beefnut, Belovedfreak, BenBaker, BesigedB, Betzalelx, BillWSmithJr, Bilybones2, BladeHamilton, Blessonbeats, Blob, Blobglob, BlueAg09, Blueyoshi321, Bobby122, Bobianite, Bobmanlea, Bobo192, Bobpenguin, Boing! said Zebedee, Bolonium, Boneheadmx, Bongwarrior, Bonked116, Boo mac, Bookofjude, BoomerAB, Breakfast machine, Brianga, Bridies, Brighterorange, Bronson, Brossow, Browntooth, Brusegadi, Brutaldeluxe, Bryan Derksen, Bsadowski1, BubaHuba, Bubbachuck, Bulgun, Bunchofgrapes, C. M. Harris, CBDunkerson, CF 444, CHRISTIANgamer97, CIreland, CJSprite, CL, CLW, CO, CQJ, CWY2190, CWii, Cactus.man, Cadsuane Melaidhrin, Cal boudicca, Calabraxthis, Caliah, Call me Bubba, Caltas, Cameron hayter1990, Camw, Can't sleep, clown will eat me, CanDo, CanadianLinuxUser, Canterbury Tail, Capix, Capricorn42, Captain Jrad420, Captain panda, Caramdir, Carlos Porto, Carmichael, CarolGray, Cassandra B, Catgut, CatherineMunro, CattleGirl, Cayzle, Cbicle, Cdpopham, Celestianpower, Centrx, Cerebellum, CesarB, Chaos5023, Charles Gaudette, Charles Matthews, Charlo blade123, Cheezermega, Chenmas229, Chillum, Chocolateboy, Chris Roy, ChrisGualtieri, Christian List, Chwoka, CiTrusD, Cielomobile, Cik, ClamDip, Closedmouth, Club penguin beta, Cmccad, Cmdrjameson, Cmw255, Coemgenus, Coll7, Coltic, CommonsDelinker, Complex (de), ComputerSherpa, Conan-san, Conan210693, Condem, Conti, ContinueWithCaution, Conversion script, Cooper892, Coroloro, Corporal Tunnel, CosineKitty, Courcelles, Crandmck, Crank dat Quan Cosby, CrazyChemGuy, Cretog8, Crossmr, Crotalus horridus, Cruxcriticorum, CryptoDerk, Cuceresc, Cuun, Cxz111, CyberSkull, Cyde, D, D4g0thur, DARTH SIDIOUS 2, DBigXray, DJMalone, DMahalko, DVD R W, Daniel 1992, Daniel Olsen, Dante Alighieri, Dark Goob, DarkAudit, Darkhorse, Darkhunger, Darkzoro, Darth Panda, Darth Who Cares777, DasBooch, Dascott, DaveGorman, Davedx, Daveliney, Davidmcclard, Davidron, Davidsss, DavisLee, Davud363000, Dbenbenn, Dca5347, Deac2012, DeadMansFilm, DebiQue, Deckiller, DeepSkyFrontier, Deerstop, Deiaemeth, Dejhuey, Dejitarob, DemonStar55, Dennis Brown, DennyColt, Depakote, DerHexer, Devilkid101, Dfrg.msc, Dgfduck, Dheaven, Dimedo, Discospinster, Dispenser, Dkamida, Dnvrfantj, DocWatson42, DocumentN, Doomsday28, DougsTech, Download, Dr.K., DrBob, DrFod, Draconus, Dracothejuggler, Draeco, DragonLord, Drakewl, Drcodyjones, Drdestiny77, DreamOfMirrors, Dreamstar1, Dreftymac, Dreish, Druidblue, Dsm56, Dsworddragon, Duel me pl0x, DurotarLord, Dyee, Dylanbrandon286, Dysepsion, EEPROM Eagle, ELNO Checking, ESkog, Edcolins, Edderso, EddieVanZant, Edgar181, Edsel, Eeksam, Ehheh, Elaragirl, Elathiel, Electrawn, EliteShnipes392, Eliz81, Elizium23, Elleachaudaucul, Elonka, Emccrckn, Emerson7, Emmick41, Emodinol, Enviroboy, Epbr123, Erianna, Eric Sandholm, Eric-Wester, Erolos, EscapingLife, Eshafoshaf, Essexmutant, Ettrig, EvaNocturna, Evercat, Everyking, Everyone Else, Eviltrance, Exarion, Excirial, Ezowietse, F, F Notebook, FTIII, Fajro, Fdssdf, Feinoha, Ferkelparade, Fiberglass Monkey, Fieari, Fieldday-sunday, Finlay McWalter, Firetrap9254, Fishdert, Fiveofakind, Flightsoffancy, Flockmeal, Fluffernutter, Foldyman, Folic Acid, Foobar, FoxCompany, Foxj, Francois77, Frankfries, Fratley, Freakofnurture, Frecklefoot, Frednotbob, FreeMorpheme, FreelanceWizard, FreplySpang, FriedMilk, Frostlion, FrozenPurpleCube, Frymaster, Fvw, Fyarae, Fyrn, GB fan, GDI Jason, GTBacchus, Galoubet, GameDiesel, GamerPro64, GamerScourge, Gardar Rurak, Gareth Griffith-Jones, Garrettmoore91, GaussTek, Gerbrant, Ghosttr, Gigogag, Gilliam, Gillvane, Gippers322, Girbgierpob, Giveaways4rs, Gjd001, Glane23, Glen, Gloce00, Gofeel, Gogo Dodo, Goobergunch, Gornly, Gosmo, GraemeL, Graham87, Green caterpillar, GreenReaper, Greeves, Greswik, Grim23, Grook Da Oger, Grunt, Gscshoyru, Gsklee, Gtrmp, Guiltyspark, Guoshun2172, Gurch, Guse, Gustavb, Gwernol, Gwwfps, Haakon, Habap, Hadal, Haipa Doragon, Haknak, Hamiltondaniel, Harlee92, Haukurth, Havok, Hbent, Helltrauma, HenkvD, Henry Flower, Hiddenfromview, Hinata, Histrion, Hola Huba, HoodedMan, Hootforum, HordeMaster, Hortinstein, Howabout1, Howcheng, Howzeman, Hu, Hubble618, HurricaneWilson, Hydrogen Iodide, IBurger2008, IRP, IW.HG, Iamblueman4, Iamien, Ian Pitchford, IanBond, Iceberg3k, Icestorm ko, Igedan, Igsky, Ihavenolife, Ilyanep, Indium, Into The Fray, Invincible Ninja, Iohannes Animosus, Iridescent, IronGargoyle, Isaac Dupree, Isis4563, Ivan Bajlo, IvarTJ, Ixfd64, J.J.Sagnella, J.delanoy, JForget, JLevi80, JNW, JSpung, JYOuyang, Jack Naven Rulez, Jagged 85, Jakex044, Jamaicanmole, James350z, Jamesontai, Jammersdublin, Janarius, Jaypark97, Jbobsully, Jeffrey Smith, JenFanOtto, Jessie881111, Jfoldmei, JiFish, Jim Douglas, Jklharris, Jklin, Jmanappl, Jmundo, JoanneB, Jockya, JodyB, JoeSmack, Joedurb, John Doe or Jane Doe, John Smythe, John smith 99, John.constantine, JohnOwens, JohnR.E.Henry, JohnnyB, JohnnyMrNinja, Johntex, Jokl, Jon186, JonasRH, Jordc1991, Josalinda, Joseph.Re, Josephs1, Josh3276, Josh7289, Joshuapaquin, JovBlackheart, Joyous!, Jpers36, Jtalledo, JuJube, Justhim00, Justin Eiler, K.Nevelsteen, KGV, KGasso, Kaid100, Kaihsu, Kaisershatner, Kanonkas, Kappa, Karada, Karen Johnson, Karimarie, Kateshortforbob, Keilana, Keith D, Kellen, Kencf0618, Kerotan, Kessler, Ketil, Kf4bdy, Khefri, Kicking222, Kill kron, Killdec, Kimera757, Kiminatheguardian, Kithric, Kjoonlee, Klcacalg, Klwalton88, Knutux, Koolkirby, Koolguy12345, Kotra, Krellis, Krinkle, Krissy718, Krun, Krustykev, Ktheory, Kukini, Kwekubo, Kx1186, Kyle Barbour, Kylu, L33tpwn4ge, LHOO, Lacon432, LadyBowN64, Larry_Sanger, Latentix, Lazulilasher, Leansmith, LeaveSleaves, Led Zeppelin129, Ledgard5060, Lennon, LentaLL, LeoNomis, LeoTimm, Lifefeed, Liftarn, Lightdarkness, Lights, Lincoln.hamilton, Livajo, Live2Love, LizardPariah, LoQon, Lockeownzj00, Lonsafko, Lord Alderaan, Lordaltay, Lotje, Louisng114, Lowellian, Lradrama, Lstanley1979, LtPowers, Lucid, Lugia2453, Luigi2, Luk, LulDIK, Lulzpwner1337, Luna Santin, Lzur, M.O.X, MER-C, MStraw, MZMcBride, MaXiMiUS, Madchester, Madjohnflint, Maestrosync, Magicevan, Mailer diablo, Makemi, Malik Shabazz, Malo, Manop, Marasmusine, Marblespire, Marcheshakker, Marcmy, Marek69, Mark Arsten, Mark rico, Masaruemoto, Masteroffogofwar, Mathmo, MattieTK, Mav, Maverickhunterx017, Maxim, Maziotis, Mbell, Mboverload, Mbroderick271, McGeddon, McLovin367, Mcfar54, Mcfly, Mckyj57, Mechasheherezada, Meekohi, Mentifisto, Micahberman, Michael Hardy, Michaelas10, Michaeldsuarez, Mikario, Mike Rosoft, Mikelr, Miko3k, Minesweeper, Minghong, Minimac, MinuteHand, Misterkillboy, Misterx2000, Miszal3, MithrandirAgain, Mkaycomputer, Mmcdougall, Mmoverload, Mnkman918, MoaM, Moberg, Modida, Modster, Moocats, Mosseman, Mr Sir Michael, MrOllie, Mrwojo, Mschlindwein, MuZemike, Mud4t, Mufka, Mugka, Munchman, Mwanner, Mxn, Mycroft7, Mylon, Myrdred, Mysdaao, Mysekurity, Mysteryquest, N432138, N5iln, NHRHS2010, NJR ZA, NLUT, NTRabbit, Nabeelo, Nagy, Nagytibi, Nahallac Silverwinds, Nakon, Natalie Erin, Nate1481, Natedog250, Nathanlee06, NawlinWiki, Ncmvocalist, Ndegrand, Necrobjon, Neil916, NerdyScienceDude, Neverquick, New Age Retro Hippie, Newsmare, Nextil, NicAgent, Nickptar, Nielspeterqm, Nifboy, Nightmaj, Nincb123, Ninly, Nk, Nneonneo, No Guru, NoIdeaNick, NoahK, Nonnb, Noommos, Norborb, Northgrove, Nuggetboy, Nunh-huh, Nyttend, OMGLOLWTF1988, Obli, Observer14, Obsessivelanguagelearner, Od Mishehu, Oj119, Oliver202, OllyG, Omfgstfun00b, Omgomgdylan, On5deu, Onebravemonkey, Oneiros, Onorem, Oooskjkd, Opelio, Orange Suede Sofa, Order of the Nameless, Orican, Ost316, Otterpops, OutRider2003, Outblood, Outriggr, Overfiend 87, OwenX, Oxymoron83, Pacs34, PadawanMD, Pagrashtak, Paliku, Pathoschild, Patriarch, Paulc206, Pb30, Peepopuppee, Penwhale, Percy Snoodle, Persian Poet Gal, Peruvianllama, Pete Iriarte, Petri Krohn, Phgao, Phil Bordelon, PhilHibbs, Philipwhiuk, Philosophistry, Phlebas, Phoenix Hacker, Piano non troppo, Picapica, Piecemealcranky, Pigman, Pilias, Pilotguy, PinchasC, PinkSock69, Pinotgris, PizzaMan, Plasticup, PlatformerMastah, Plutochaun, Pne, Pnm, Pockle, PoliticalJunkie, Ponder, Poopyflu38, Poor Yorick, Postwar, Prabash.A, Printspike, Prithwis, Prodego, Prolog, Propower, Protonk, PseudoSudo, Psy guy, Psychochild, Puddhe, PureSkillGaming, Pxma, Qboroking, QuagmireDog, Quentonamos, Question2, Quoth, Qwyrxian, Qxz, RFAronson, RG2, RHB, RJFJR, RS Ren, Radon210, RainbowOfLight, Raiyea, Rambutaan, Rampart, Random user 39849958, Random832, Rasmus Faber, Ratiocinate, Ravenswing, Rawbanana, Rayzor, Razimus, Rbb138, Realko, Reaper Eternal, RebeccaMAdcox, Reedy, Reelrt, Reintb, Renedrivers, Reneeholle, Reredrose, Rev22, RexNL, ReyBrujo, Rfighter, Rfl, Rginns, Rhobite, Rhunedhel, Rich Farmbrough, Richard D. LeCour, RichardF, Richterks, Ricky81682, Riden1000, Rigadoun, Rixgaming, Rl, Roara, RobertG, Rocio Nadat, RockMFR, Rockfang, Rocktacity, Roflcopter, Roozbenjrox, RoyBoy, Royalleegend, Royin345, Rror, Rsw, Rubyrocks, Rukifellth, RuneFire, Runefurb, Runtime, Russoc4, Rv2000wiki, RxS, Ryan Paddy, Ryan032, Ryulong, S0me l0ser, SG 01, SJP, SJennings, SMC, SWAdair, Salvio giuliano, Sam 1123, Samdod2427, Samuel Levine, Samwalton9, San de Berg, Sango123, Satori Son, Savidan, Sayden, Scepia, Sceptre, SchfiftyThree, Sciurinæ, Scoops, Scottj017, Sct72, Seancdaug, Secretlondon, Seduisant, Seeonee, Sellyme, Seltar, Senator Palpatine, Sepper, Serein (renamed because of SUL), Serendipodous, Sesshomaru, Shadow Swampland, Shadowlynk, Shaffali, Shanel, SharkD, ShawnVW, Shawnc, Sherurcij, Shinpah1, Shruti14, Silver Edge, SilverLancer, SimonP, Sin-man, SiobhanHansa, SirBruce, Sirius81, Siyavash, Slashme, SlipperyHippo, Slowcooker55, Sm8900, Smithers7, Smm11235, Smokizzy, Snagari, SnowFire, Soliloquial, Solitude, Sopher99, SoulAngel, Sourside21, SoylentGreenEater, SpaceFlight89, Sparky the Seventh Chaos, SparrowsWing, Specs112, Specter01010, Splamo, Splintax, Squids and Chips, Squirrel Killer, Staceysavage1991, Staka, Stapleymas229, Steel, Steelaxe, StefanDasbach, Stephan Leeds, Stepheno, Steve898989, Stoneice02, Stopqq, Stradden, Studerby, StudySage, SubSeven, SuperSmashBros.Brawl777, Superbeecat, Supparluca, Suprtigr, Svippong, Svntnth, Sykobronco, Syvanen, T-dog5457, THEN WHO WAS PHONE?, TKD, TPMX, Tabletop, Tadas12, Tal Baron, Tanaats, Tangotango, Tarinth, Tarnum, Tasowiki, TastyPoutine, Tawker, Tbhotch, Tearbleu, Tedrick79, Tehbuttcheeksfairy, Telamon, Teokk, Tetris325, TexMurphy, Texture, Tgeairn, Th1rt3en, Thanumber1killaz, The Captain Returns, The Man13, The REAL Dyslexic Q-Thief, The Rambling Man, The Thing That Should Not Be, The demiurge, The undertow, The1337gamer, The93owner, TheDotGamer, TheGreenMartian, TheIncredibleEdibleOompaLoompa, TheJazzDalek, TheKMan, TheKoG, TheNewPhobia, TheSpectator, TheTrojanHought, TheYmode, Thealternativescott, Thehelpfulone, Themalau, Themfromspace, Themoodyblue, Theodolite, Thingg, Thiseye, Thsms204, Tide rolls, TigerShark, TimVickers, Timberlax, Timbo123456789, Titoxd, Tktktk, Tomdatom, Tomgdoe16, Tommy11111, Tommy2010, Tomwalden, Tony1, Toussaint, Tracy Guile, Trampl122, Transformers666, Treksbated, Trevor MacInnis, Trijnstel, Trinexx, Triwbe, Trlkly, Trollyomama, Truthflux, Truthmaster0, Trystan, Tubby, Tuxide, Tvinh, TwistOfCain, Tymon18, U.S.A.U.S.A.U.S.A., Ubertionary, Uncle Dick, Unknowman21, Unsterblich, Unusualsuspects, Unzinc, Useight, Username550, Uucp, Vanished User 1004, Vardion, Vcelloho, VegKilla, Velella, Venorik, Versus22, Victory93, Vina, Vincent Lextrait, Violetriga, Vorik111, Vranak, Vyxx, WAS 4.250, WOW, Wafulz, Wahooker, Waldir, Walkiped, WarhammerOnlinesupport, WastBarktender100, Watemark, Werdan7, Wes dude, Wesley, West.andrew.g, WhiteDragon, Widr, Wiggleintatter, Wiki alf, Wiki-Ed, Wiki461, WikiDan61, WikipedianMarlith, Wikipelli, Wildcats087, WillDarlock, Wimt, Windchaser, Winhunter, Winterheart, Wirbelwind, Wittylama, Wlievens, Woodroar, Woohookitty, Wootking, Wormywyrm, Wrinkle, Wsiegmund, X!, X201, XXdeath55XX, XXidiotXx, Xanzzibar, Xect, Xela Yrag, Xeno, Xezbeth, Xinit, Xneilj, Xnuala, Xranthoius, Xrrgaming, Xxmosesxx, Xymostech, Yamaguchi, Yamamoto Ichiro, Yelyos, Yerpo, Yintan, Yobb, Yushiyang, Z897623, Zac2333, Zalgo, Zanimum, Zarex, ZayZayEM, Ze miguel, Zeno McDohl, Zerath13, Zirkov, Zoe, Zoicon5, Zro, Zzubiri, Zzuuzz, 2936 anonymous edits

EverQuest *Source*: http://en.wikipedia.org/w/index.php?title=EverQuest *Contributors*: 12.224.56.xxx, 24fan24, 62.253.64.xxx, 6birc, A. Swearengen, AJay17, AKM, Aaronw, Addit, Aeonite, Aeroknight, Aezka, Ahasuerus, Ajm81, Ajshm, Akc370, Alansohn, Alerante, AlienRage, Alphachimp, Altzinn, Andrewgameinsight, AndrogenousAndy, Angela, Anirluph, AnnaFrance,

Anonymous101, Antandrus, Antondb, Arch5280, Arnoox, Arthena, Astanhope, Atarimark, Avsa, Awesomerface, Axem Titanium, Azxten, Badanedwa, Baeritone, Bagatelle, Ballstastegood, BananaFiend, BankBank, Barek, Barliner, Belovedfreak, Benjiballin, Bhauk, Bholloway, Bilbo571, Billimek, Binary TSO, Bkellihan, Bkonrad, Blackdog5703, BlakOut, Bob A, Bob98133, Bobblewik, Bobo192, Bobog, Bongwarrior, Bookuser, Bounder10, Brazil4Linux, Brianga, Brianreading, Bschueler2, C mon, Cadsuane Melaidhrin, Caltas, Can't sleep, clown will eat me, Candorwien, CanisRufus, Capsela, CarTick, Catgut, Chaos5023, Charles Matthews, ChaseBilleaudeau, Chipmunk01, Chris the speller, ChrisGualtieri, ChrisWright1979, Christopher Parham, Cielomobile, Cjwright79, Ckatz, Clayoquot, Clokverkorange, Cloud83, Clueless, Cmdrjameson, Codetiger, Colincbn, Colorfast, Comatose51, CommonsDelinker, Conversion script, Cooliodefabio, Courtf, CrazyChemGuy, Crossmr, Crowless, Cthompson, CyberShadow, CyberSkull, Cynical, Czaemon, D, D6, DXBari, DangerousPotential, Dca5347, Deathowl, Dedcreature123, Dedcreaturea1234, Derfy, Dev93l, Dgwai, Diannaa, Dimbob, Dispenser, DocWatson42, Dominic, Dominick, Donknottso, Doulos Christos, Downwardone, DrButyl, DragonReader, Drat, Drazzminius, Dreadstar, Drogan101, Dureo, DustJesus, ECHphotonic, EEPROM Eagle, Edgar181, Ee79, Eekerz, Ehheh, El levine, Elenseel, Elfguy, Eluchil, EmmyMaven, Emnar, Engelcox, Epbr123, Eqlover, Everquestor, Eviltrance, Excirial, Explicit, Ezhar Fairlight, Ezra Wax, F3RR4L, Father Inire, Favonian, Finngall, Flipkin, FlooK, Floppie, FlyxCutlery, Fordsbasement, Fram, Freakmighty, Frecklefoot, FrisoHoltkamp, Froth, Frybread, Fxmercenary, Gail, Gamelore, Gargaj, GateKeeper, GavinJenkins, Gebharra, GentlemanGhost, Gerrish, Gk007, Glane23, Gogo Dodo, Golbez, GraemeL, Greldon, Griffinofwales, Griimory, GundamsRus, Guox0032, Hairchrm, HalfShadow, Hargael, Harmil, Hashar, Hazzardlampshade, Hede2000, Hells Malice, Hoovie, Horst F JENS, I do not exist, InfiniteCenturion, Ingolfson, Islandboy99, Isomorphic, It Is Me Here, J-Ros, J.delanoy, JacDT, Jadams, Jckheather, Jcmiller67, Jeff Alexander, Jeffanthonyfds, Jeremyb, Jestix, Jfowler27, Jidar, Jiy, Jj137, JoDOe, John of Reading, JohnInDC, Johnleemk, Johnlm01, Johntex, Jonmilby, Jopickard, Joseph Dwayne, Jotraynor, Jrdioko, Justie1220, Jxm, K, K1Bond007, Kajolus, Kamic, Karatenerd, Kazin Kagari, Kazvorpal, Kbh3rd, Keegan, Keeper76, Keithustus, KhatNip, KingTT, Klow, KnightRider, Koavf, Kurrupt3d, Kx1186, Kylven, Larry_Sanger, Lars Washington, Latka, Live2Love, Llort, Loodog, Loremaster, Lstanley1979, LtPowers, Lukemaitland, MSJapan, Madeleined2, Magu2k, Mandarax, Mantees, MarSch, Marsilies, Martarius, MarydaleEd, Master Thief Garrett, Master of Puppets, Mathmo, Matthewbisanzisaslut, Maximus Rex, Mboverload, McGriddles, Meeples, Melander, Memex, Merenta, Mewcenary, Michaelbolland, Michaellikespoop, Michaelmike147, Mika1h, Mike Payne, MiloDC, MindstormsKid, Mithrandr12345, Modemac, Moeron, Moink, Momex2000, Moonriddengirl, Mrdice, Mrwojo, Mshea, Mspraveen, Musical Linguist, Mygerardromance, Mysidia, N0valyfe1, Nahallac Silverwinds, Nbm589, Nerd101010, New Age Retro Hippie, NightBear, Nizer, No Guru, Nolrog, NorsemanII, NuclearWarfare, Olathe, Omicronpersei8, Onorem, Ootachi, Oscarthecat, Overload Capacity, Oyeahiitisidat, PGWG, Pdfpdf, Percy Snoodle, Permanentbliss, Peter Winnberg, Pgcdan, Pgk, Pharaoh of the Wizards, Phil Sandifer, Philip Trueman, PhilipO, PhishPhan143, Phl3djo, Pilotguy, Pne, Poiuyt Man, Primalmoon, Protonk, Psychochild, Putonformycity, Quotison, Qxx, RUL3R, Raioke, Rakonas, RasputinAXP, Raven4x4x, Ravimakkar, Rawrzorzor, Razielsr, Razr Nation, Rcherrick, ReCover, Reikazen, Retropunk, Richardcavell, Rjbouchard, Rjo, Rjwilmsi, RockMFR, RolandTheHeadlessThompsonGunner, Ron google, Ryūkotsusei, S@bre, SBKT, SYSS Mouse, Salavat, Salvio giuliano, Sam Hocevar, Samanna, Sarrene, Sbluen, SchfiftyThree, Sdornan, Sethie, ShadowKatmandu, Shajure, Shannara, Shawnc, Sietse Snel, SimonD, Simonfl, Simplefishman, Sjc, Skippy1999, Smitty, Snazster, Soap, Soetermans, Some guy, Spencer.fry@yale.edu, Spidey104, Spiffulent, Spitfire, SpuriousQ, Stapleman, Stelker, Steven Zhang, Steveprutz, Sticky Light, Stonehook, Stormie, Strom, Sue Rangell, Sullivan.t, Swift, Syrthiss, TAP3AH, TJ Spyke, TKD, Tabletop, Tarc, Technogeek, Terrapin, Terukiyo, The Cool Kat, The Corruption of Lol, The Haunted Angel, The Thing That Should Not Be, The1337gamer, TheRedPenOfDoom, Theavatar3, Thebisch, Thibbs, Thingg, Throwaway85, Thumperward, Tide rolls, Timothyc123, Topbanana, TransUtopian, Tree Biting Conspiracy, Tregoweth, Turlo Lomon, Twas Now, Ukulele, Uncle G, Unionhawk, UnknownToa, Unuca, Vanished User 1004, Vary, Veesicle, VegaDark, Veinor, Velella, Verbal, Versus22, Victory93, Vince192837465, Vivio Testarossa, Vranak, Wakawakapukapaka, WalkinDownThirtyThree, Washburnmav, Weaponking, Who, Wickethewok, Wiki alf, Wikibob, Wikidenizen, Wikipelli, Will Beback Auto, Wimt, Windkin, Wmahan, Woohookitty, X-factor, Xanzzibar, Xbiggio7x, Y0u, Ylva Vargdotter, Zachary emami, Zachd20130203390852, Zaharous, Zehanonimo, Zmajc, Zoggie50, Ævar Arnfjörð Bjarmason, 1098 anonymous edits

Warhammer_Online:_Age_of_Reckoning *Source*: http://en.wikipedia.org/w/index.php?title=Warhammer_Online:_Age_of_Reckoning *Contributors*: -OOPSIE-, 3toe, 4drenalin3, A ufie, A*-search, A3RO, Aanhorn, Ab.er.rant, Admiral Stark, Aekos, Ahkond, Aibyou chan, Alansohn, Alien1099, Alitheas, Allstarecho, Andy M. Wang, Animediter, ArchonMagnus, ArglebargleIV, Arsenik, Ary29, Ashkenazzi, Asosocrates, Asplosion, AtomicDog1471, Ausir, BALCKORK, Bart133, Bartledan, Bearcat, Beejhou, Behindcurtain3, Blehfu, Bob, Bobbyroana, Bobo192, Bobosdkk, Bonadea, Boreas74, Bowsy, Bradeos Graphon, Breezermajic, Bultro, CaelumArisen, Caidh, Call me ishmail, Campbellce, CapnZapp, CardinalDan, ChaosAkita, Chase me ladies, I'm the Cavalry, ChazzK, ChunkySoup, Closedmouth, Corellion, Credema, Ctbolt, Cube2000, Cybercobra, Cynric35, CzarB, Dabomb87, Daersun, Damos247, Dark984, Davedude2040, Deadplayer, Demo2000, Denton22, DerHexer, Dfrg.msc, Discospinster, Dizzam, Djarudiin, Douglasr007, Drakesable, Dreamyrider, EEMIV, Elthiria, Endo-Plexor, Epbr123, Etaew, Etincelles, Everyking, Eviltrance, Exander, Excirial, Failgasm, Falcon4196, Falcorian, Faramir1138, Faustuss, Fireguardiantmnt, Flewis, Fourthords, Foxfoil, Fr0, FritzG, Frostlion, Funforall666, Gaius Cornelius, GamerPro64, Garth 187, Giraffedata, Gizzakk, Gloce00, GoodDamon, GraemeLeggett, Granf, Greg Douglas, Gundato, Hazmo1, Helot50, Hirmetrium, Hobartimus, HorusRising882, Hydrogen Iodide, Idragona, Ifrit, Igno2, Ilkali, Imhoteppen, Itanius, J.D Rankin, J.delanoy, J.smith, JDspeeder1, JHunterJ, JL096, JaGa, Jack's Revenge, Jackdays, Jdengler, Jeff G., Jelloollej, JerrySteal, Jjthewonderboy, Jlahorn, John Doe or Jane Doe, Johnanth, Joshmaul, JustAGal, Kagetto, Kainouss, Kallimina, Kaod, Karlschenk, Katharineamy, Kawaii-Soft, Knowledgeum, KoalaMeatPie, Kraftlos, KriticKill, Kurrurrin, KyleWells, Kylven, LHOO, Lacon432, Lahiru k, Landon1980, LarianLeQuella, LeaveSleaves, LightI3ulb, Lingfu, Lloydiboi, Loonetik, Lord Alderaan, Lord Hawk, Lord Migraine, Loren.wilton, LttS, Lucas Murray, M0rphz, MBisanz, MC10, MER-C, Magozar, Malcolmxl5, Martarius, Matthewjbarnard, Meaghan, Meandyourmum, Mefanch, Mentifisto, Mika1h, Miquonranger03, Mister Victor, MrOllie, Mtking, MuZemike, Musicacbx, Mygerardromance, N. Harmonik, N0f3ai2, Nalatkal, Nayl, Nazgum, Neelix, Next-Genn-Gamer, Nikkip00t, Nleseul, NuclearWarfare, Nucleusboy, Nymf, Od Mishehu, Odie5533, Ohconfucius, Ohnoitsjamie, Omicronpersei8, OpeneyesZZZZ, Oscarthecat, Oxymoron83, PacPomarnacki, Paperfire, PennyWhistle99, Pentasyllabic, Persian Poet Gal, Petesmiles, Pewpew, Pharaoh of the Wizards, Philip Trueman, Phrenology, Piggyjon382, PowerNoise, Pred, Protonk, Quaeler, RJHall, Raignn, RainbowOfLight, Ralff, Rasmasyean, Ravenhull, Red Director, Redd Dragon, Redmond Barry, Reedy, Reikazen, Retry90, Revolutionesque, Revoranii, ReyBrujo, Rhaka, Rjwilmsi, Robomaeyhem, Ron Ritzman, Ronhjones, Rror, Ryulong, SJP, SQL, ST47, STLocutus, Satori Son, Schuitild, Scirex, Sct72, SeTiDaYeTi, Secretplat, Senator Palpatine, Sgtjoo, SharkD, Sharkface217, Shrumster, Sidhebolg, Siloria, Silver Edge, Simoes, SimonD, Simplefishman, Skapunkmetalskater, SkyWalker, Snareshot, SoWhy, Solitude, Sophia™, Sophus Bie, Spikeynorman, SpinachConvention, Sqren, Staecker, Stenitzer, Stormscape, Strythium, Suncrafter, Sykskar, Taelus, TaintedMustard, Tarinth, Tasoli, Tcoop978, Teancum, Tere123123, Tetsuox, TexMurphy, The Merciful, TheCommodore7, TheGrimReaper NS, TheKoG, Thehealeroftru, Theplumber10, Threedots dead, Thumperward, Tide rolls, Tindanian, TomStar81, Tony1, Tornvmax, Trainra, Travin18, Twas Now, Tyjoru, Tylerdmace, Tyrtamus, Una Smith, Unicityd, VI, Vanished User 1004, Vanished user uih38riiw4hjlsd, Versus22, Victory93, Videmus Omnia, Vishnava, Volomon, WadeSimMiser, WanderSage, Wargod316, WarhammerOnlinesupport, WereSpielChequers, Wiki Roxor, WikipedianMarlith, Wingsandsword, Wrel, Xxavyer, Yamamoto Ichiro, Yaris678, Ye Editor, Zarex, Zeix50, Zhanghia, Zinjixmaggir, ZombieDev, Τασουλα, 1315 anonymous edits

namespace:The dot-com bubble in the United States *Source*: http://en.wikipedia.org/w/index.php?title=Dot-com_bubble *Contributors*: 0, 0sd9gj0s9:D:D, 15.112, 159753, 213.253.39.xxx, 2bar, 99econ, A2-computist, ABCOffice.com, Academic Challenger, Adam.ambrozewicz, Adamfinmo, Airplaneman, Akamad, Alansohn, AlexWangombe, Alexander lau, Alexburnsdisinfo, AlistairMcMillan, Amatulic, Amcfreely, Anastrophe, Ancheta Wis, Andrew Gwilliam, Andrew.auerbach, Andyabides, Angela, Ankursh, Antaeus Feldspar, Antarctica moon, Anthony Appleyard, Aranel, Artem Karimov, Arthena, Astronautics, Auroranorth, Autopilots, Avsa, BD2412, Badger Drink, Bazj, Bedya, Bender235, Benstrider, Bhny, BigT27, Billhpike, Bizzwriter, BlackDeath3, BlackTerror, Blahcake666, Bobblewik, Bobmack89x, Bolwerk, Brennan626, BrokenSegue, Brownsteve, Bryan Derksen, Btyner, Budgy Speedwagon, Byelf2007, Calltech, Carina22, Casito, Cdc, Centrx, CesarB, Cflm001, Chabuk, Chill Pill Bill, Chowbok, Chris Capoccia, ChrisBaker, ChrisGualtieri, ChrisRuvolo, Chubdub, Cjkporter, Cmdrjameson, Colonies Chris, Compfreak7, Connelly, Coolcaesar, Corn cheese, CplSmugleaf, Cretog8, CrunchRaisin, Csteinb, Curtdbz, Cyanoa Crylate, DEddy, DJAyres, DMCer, Da7sm0, DabMachine, Dale Arnett, Darkuranium, Dashkoff, Davejenk1ns, Daverocks, David Gerard, DavidLevinson, Dbenbenn, Ddgromit, Ddxc, DecadeMan, Deiz, Dept of Alchemy, Dewritech, Dissident, Djegan, Djournal, Doc Strange, DocendoDiscimus, Doggie Yum Yums, Dolovis, Donner60, Doradus, DreamGuy, Drmagic, Dylan Lake, EconomistBR, Ed Poor, Ed g2s, Editor at Large, Edward, Effer, ElCharismo, Emurphy42, Esperant, Eugene-elgato, Eurosong, Everyking, Ewlyahoocom, FFMG, Fellinox, Ferkelparade, Fig wright, Firsfron, Flodded, Flyerhell, Flygon, Fmjohnson, Foober, Francesdeleon, Fratley, Frecklefoot, Fredrik, Froth, Frothy, Funandtrvl, Fuper, Gazpacho, Gdo01, Geni, Gibson Flying V, Giftlite, Gioto, Golbez, Goudzovski, GraemeL, Grenavitar, Grick, Guroadrunner, Guy Harris, GyaroMaguus, Gyrofrog, H.al-shawaf, HaeB, Haeinous, Hailey C. Shannon, Hairy Dude, Haku8645, HeinzzzderMannn, Henning Makholm, Hephaestos, Hmains, Hope(N Forever), Howcheng, Htournyol, Hyad, Internetstartups, InverseHypercube, Isnow, It's the economy, Ixfd64, Izhukov, J matula, JAF1970, JRSpriggs, James084, JanSuchy, Jaraalbe, Jburt1, Jeffsmo, Jerek Deter, Jerryseinfeld, Jimp, Jinf22, Jmreinhart, JoanneB, Joefromrandb, JohnOwens, Joonneess, Joseph Solis in Australia, Jpatokal, Jrinaldi97, Jrintanen, Kchampcal, Kchaox, Kennedye, Khym Chanur, Kumioko (renamed), Kurowoofwoof111, Kvasi, Kzzl, L'omo del batocio, LLMMScMa, LachlanA, Lalala666, Lamro, Larry V, LeeHunter, Lemmey, LeoO3, LesmanaZimmer, LifeStar, Lifefeed, Little Professor, Llavigne, Lokicarbis, LuK3, Lysdexia, M. E. Smith, M0RHI, MCSKY, MER-C, MPS, Macrakis, Magnum87, Mailer diablo, Makemi, Mamizou, Maproom, Marcus Qwertyus, Marian Dan, Mark Millard, Martarius, Matdrodes, Matt Deres, MattTM, Mattis, Maxim Masiutin, Melsaran, Melvalevis, Merglee, Mfb52, Michael Hardy, Mig21bp, Mikcob, Mikhail Ryazanov, Minesweeper, Miterdale, Modster, Monkeyman, Mordgier, Morning277, Mowsbury, Mr30, Mrwojo, Mschlindwein, Mydogategodshat, Myriad, NJgeezer, NTDOY Fanboy, Nabeth, Naudefj, Nealcardwell, Neelix, Nemalki, Neocapitalist, Neutrality, Ngebendi, Nigelj, Nighend, Night Gyr, Night Ranger, Nightstallion, Nikai, Niteowlneils, Nky, No1lakersfan, NuclearWarfare, Nukethewales, OccamzRazor, Olivier, Omicronpersei8, Omnipaedista, Orcar967, Orpheus, Overboard, Padillah, Pakaran, PanMan, Pashute, Patandgreg, Peyre, Pgp688, Pgreenfinch, Philip Trueman, Piano non troppo, Plutor, Polylerus, ProfessorPaul, ProhibitOnions, Pseudomonas, Quadell, Quadra630, R Lowry, R3m0t, Ragan651, Rapsar, Rasmus Faber, Razorflame, Raztus, Rdsmith4, Rechta, RedWolf, Reedy, Res2216firestar, Retired username, Revolutionary, RexNL, Reywas92, Rgoodermote, Rich Farmbrough, Riverwildcat, Rjwilmsi, Rnickel, Robert Merkel, Romanski, RoyBoy, Rspeer, Rujo91, S.K., SMC, Samsara, Samwb123, Sanchezman, Sandyiit, Saros136, Savidan, Scarlett8188, Seigneur101, Sfoerster, Shanedidona, Signocom, SimonP, Sinisterscrawl, SiobhanHansa, Sitenl, Skew-t, Skybunny, Slady, Slightsmile, Sm8900, Smb1138, Smoovement, Smyth, Soerfm, Solphusion, SparrowsWing, Speciate, Speer320, Srich32977, Standardfact, Stanton5, Steve Dufour, Stevenmitchell, Steverapaport, Stevietheman, Stirling Newberry, Stormwatch, Subwayguy, Suisui, Supertouch, Suslindisambiguator, Sven Manguard, Syferus, TCO, TNLNYC, TPIRFanSteve, TakuyaMurata, Tapir Terrific, Tassedethe, Taxman, Tazzaler, Tempshill, TerraFrost, ThaddeusB, TheAbsoluteTruth, TheInformationist, TheSeer, Thebt, Thefixerupers, Thelyrical42, Thijs en, Thomas Paine1776, Tim!, Timwi, Tinalandrith, Tkynerd, Tommy2010, Tparaiso, Tpbradbury, Trainthh, TreboniusArtorius, Tregoweth, Trek011, Trivialist, Tuxlie, TwoTwoHello, UTboyprobs, UnitedStatesian, Unregistered.coward, Urbane Legend, Uucp, Vanished user 5zariu3jisj0j4irj, Velella, Verbose, Viriditas, Voidxor, VoluntarySlave, W163, Wavelength, Waycool27, Wayne Slam, Wayward, WhisperToMe, Whomp, Widr, WikHead, Wisdom89, Wtmitchell, Xeltran, Xtifr, Yamamoto Ichiro, Ylem, Zorakoid, Zyxwv99, Фрай, 661 anonymous edits

Square_Enix *Source*: http://en.wikipedia.org/w/index.php?title=Square_Enix *Contributors*: 041744, 2600:1012:B00B:6194:F064:375A:2D8:F57, 3cheesed, A Man In Black, Addihockey10, Adimovk5, Aeonx, Alasdair, Almightypical, Amren, Andrevan, Anibas, Anniv22, Ansend, Antster1983, Antunesi, Apostrophe, Aresmo, Arrowny, Aspects, Assassingod, Axem Titanium, B-RadShock3, BD2412, Banej, BattleMario, Bbatsell, Benjamin Soltani, Bilbo571, Bishop13, Blade Hirato, Bluerfn, Bobo192, Bongwarrior, Bradleyjx, Buckeyes1186, Caleb5617, Camembert, Can't sleep, clown will eat me, CanadianLinuxUser, Captainrag, CaseyPenk, Casper10, Centrx, Charitwo, Chocobogamer, Chris the speller, Chronodm, Chupon, Cloud668, Combination,

Commander Shepard, CommonsDelinker, Contributor777, Crevox, CyberSkull, Cyborg Ninja, DAJF, DH85868993, DJ WhiteC, DKqwerty, Da D00d Uploader, Daggoth, Dan Fuhry, DarkEvil, Darkhunger, Darkishblade, Darranc, Datrio, Deckiller, Decltype, DerHexer, DisneyGirlovestacos1995, Dispenser, DoubleCross, DraQue Star, Dreaded Walrus, Dyreschlock, Eggman183, ElKevbo, Endlos 669, Enixx, Enterryan, Erlik.khan, Evanh2008, Everyking, Evice, Exukvera, Exult, Eyesnore, Fang Aili, Farine, Favonian, Feral-Golduck, Fewmenleft, Fg2, Fiftyquid, FightingStreet, Final Fan Daisy, Fixer88, Flipkin, Flooey, Foobar, Fractyl, Frank, Frecklefoot, Funnysheep, G-Zay, GG Crono, Gabe1972, GaeMFreeK, Gaius Cornelius, GameboyMad, Geg, Gogo Dodo, GoingBatty, Golbez, Gordon Ecker, Gp nintendo, GreaterWikiholic, Greenshed, GrumpyTroll, Gscshoyru, Gurch, Guyinblack25, Hairouna, Halestone200, HalfShadow, HappyInGeneral, Hariharan91, Harryboyles, Hibana, Hiruko, Hooverbag, Hope(N Forever), Hotjock, Hrundi Bakshi, Huangp, HunterXIV, Husond, Icep, Iggy402, Ignis33, Igordebraga, In Defense of the Artist, Inuboy1000, J Milburn, JQF, JS-Tactics, JackSparrow Ninja, Jacoplane, Jagged 85, JamieSI, Japanman93, Jayron32, Jeriaska, JiFish, Jim1138, JimmyBlackwing, Jinnai, John of Reading, JohnnyMrNinja, Jonathan Hardin', Joshg253, Journ, Jpark3909, Juhachi, Jusjih, Kaijucole, Kariteh, Kelakagandy, Kelvinc, Kerotan, Kgarr, Khsater, KiasuKiasiMan, Kkm010, Koavf, Kricxjo, Kuru, Kusunose, Kyrios320, L1amfr1zzell, La Pianista, Lacon432, LainEverliving, Lamro, Larsinio, Leandrod, Lemaroto, Lightlowemon, Lightmouse, Lil Ripsta, Lilac Soul, Logan, Lone Guardian, Lord Kestrel, Lord Pistachio, Lord Sanjuro, Magicperson6969, Magnum2037, Malcolmxl5, Mallerd, Martarius, Master Deusoma, Matiash, Mauler90, Mechturk, Megata Sanshiro, Melaen, Mentifisto, Michael Friedrich, Micmoo, Minna Sora no Shita, Mintleaf, Mog90044, Monkeymanman, Montrealais, Mps, Mrwojo, Msikma, MuffinPi, Muralsmetaphors, Mushroom, MusikAnimal, Myanw, NawlinWiki, Neelix, Neji56565onyoutube, Nifboy, Nihonjoe, NikePlus, NikkCox, Nintendomagazine, Nintendonly, Nitro DG, Nogburt, Nomchan, Notclive, Okami11, One, Oo64eva, Optichan, Oscara, Ost316, Pcyhan215, Pdiddyjr, Perfectblue97, Philip Trueman, Pie4all88, Piecemealcranky, Pikku, Pixelanteninja, Poetnk, Pointillist, PresN, Prodclod, ProtoDrake, Pseudo Intellectual, Pukstpr12, PureLegend, R'n'B, Raamin, Racklever, RadiantAmbition, RainbowOfLight, Raito89, Rakukojin, Randall Brackett, Rangoon11, Redlioness, Redryno23, Regancy42, RenamedUser01302013, Renegade Zero, Renegadeviking, Reverse polish, Rhonin the wizard, Rich Farmbrough, Rich257, Richard Meeks, Richiekim, Rjwilmsi, Rmosler2100, Roambassador, RobertG, Rockman-X, Ronark, Runningfridgesrule, Ryuukuro, SDC, SYSS Mouse, Salvio giuliano, Sauvastika, ScottJ, Seancdaug, Shadowjams, ShakingSpirit, Shortride, Sillent DX, Silver Edge, SilverKiento, Sinner145, Sjones23, SkyWalker, Smash, Sorazora, Soumyasch, Split, Squall 5387, Squally, Sufid, Suisui, Surv1v4l1st, SynergyBlades, TJ Spyke, TK, TaerkastUA, Tails0600, Tavatar, Tbhotch, Tcncv, Tedius Zanarukando, Tehw1k1, Teles, Teresa44, That Guy, From That Show!, The Light6, The Stick Man, The Thing That Should Not Be, TheBilly, TheGrimReaper NS, TheSmuel, TheSuave, TheWeakWilled, Thebelltree, Theprophet08, Thunderbrand, Tim Auke Kools, Time for action, Tom X. Tobin, Tombraiderlegend1231, Tristam, Trongphu, Trut-h-urts man, TubularWorld, TyA, Unstable ISOtope, Unused000702, Username314, Velella, Vendettax, W Tanoto, Wakuseino, WarChild, WhisperToMe, Wiz-Pro3, X201, XIChaosIX, Xeroxxx, Xiomicronpi, Yakiv Gluck, Yas, Yellow Mage, Yiiipeee, YogaWP, Yogza, Yottamol, Zachmb9, ZakuSage, Zenithian, Zeta26, Zidane4028, 959 anonymous edits

Thottbot *Source*: http://en.wikipedia.org/w/index.php?title=Thottbot *Contributors*: Andreona, Andrew Maiman, Antandrus, Antimon, Bangbangmafia, Bilby, Blanchardb, Bovlb, Chaosmagicko, CyberSkull, Darkwind, Enviroboy, FangzofBlood, Fourthords, Gary King, Gourra, Headbomb, Ioeth, Izno, JavaTenor, Judgesurreal777, KanjiNinja, Leithp, Lomn, Martinimix, McRed, MoraSique, Muchclag, Nivix, Pacman420, Pixelface, Plastikspork, Queuequeue, Robofish, Rror, SharkD, Slant, Stormbay, Tony1, Torte, Watchsmart, X201, Xezbeth, Xiong Chiamiov, Yngvarr, 50 anonymous edits

Wowhead *Source*: http://en.wikipedia.org/w/index.php?title=Wowhead *Contributors*: Amalas, Ameliorate!, Clarkcj12, Closedmouth, Conningcris, Cordless Larry, Credema, CyberSkull, DanielPharos, Davejohnsan, DerHexer, DropDeadGorgias, Father Chaos, Headbomb, Izno, Jerry, John Nevard, LFaraone, Merxistan, NMChico24, Neurolysis, Nicnik92, Pek, Protonk, Rjwilmsi, RockMFR, RoyBoy, Rwalker, Sandstein, SharkD, Taelus, Warcraftdojo, WolfyB, X201, 34 anonymous edits

Slashdot *Source*: http://en.wikipedia.org/w/index.php?title=Slashdot *Contributors*: -- April, 141.154.254.xxx, 144.132.75.xxx, 212.209.125.xxx, 2601:D:380:B5:2466:B1EA:738D:41C8, 4lex, 65.8.239.xxx, A hard won dollar, A.Kurtz, A333, ATLBeer, AVRS, Aberdeen angus, Abqwildcat, Acb, Accountagery, Adidas, Ahoerstemeier, Aisotton, Alba7, Alerante, Alexfiles, Ali K, Alphachimp, AltGrendel, Althepal, AmaryllisGardener, Amorymeltzer, Ampedup, Android Mouse, AndyHedges, Angela, Anonymous 57, Anonymous Andy, Anonymous Dissident, Anonymous3190, Anthony Appleyard, Anticipation of a New Lover's Arrival, The, Arensb, Arfur pinta lager, Arisa, Arj, Armaced, Armbrust, Arrenlex, Arthena, Arvindn, Aryonoco, Asbestos, Autocracy, Axl, Axlq, Ayecee, Azquelt, BBird, BW, Badbadtimez, Balajiviswanathan, BalooUrsidae, Banzai!, Bdesham, Bedders, Benhall2121, Betacommand, Beverage base, orange, Bevo, Bierwurst, BigKaboom2, Billlava, Boarder8925, BobDively, Bobo192, Bogdangiusca, Bonadea, Booyabazooka, Bramlet Abercrombie, Brianicus, BrokenSegue, Brucevdk, Brusk, Bryan Derksen, Btw0, Buddy13, BullRangifer, CCFreak2K, Cachedio, Cacophony, Calimo, Calmypal, Can't sleep, clown will eat me, CanadianCaesar, Captain rockhead, Castle of ortsacx, Causa sui, Celf4444, Celsius1414, CesarB, Cgs, Chaojoker, CharlotteWebb, CharonX, Chayama, Chealer, Chmod007, ChristTrekker, Christiant, Christopher Kraus, Christopher Mahan, Church of emacs, Ciphergoth, Civlov, Claviola, Clinton Baptiste, Closeapple, Conversion script, Coolotter88, CrazyRob926, Createur, Crewcut, Crossmr, Crystallina, Curps, CzarB, Czj, DJ John, DMacks, DXBari, DaB., DaGizza, Dabomb87, Dalmiroy2k, Damian Yerrick, Damiens.rf, Danieyek, DavidWBrooks, Dawnseeker2000, Dbchip, Dcclark, Deggir reggin, Delirium, Delorme, Deltabeignet, Demus Wiesbaden, Denelson83, Dennis Brown, Denoir, Derek.cashman, Dguido, Diehardtrekkie, Dkrogers, Dlohcierekim, Dmgultekin, DocWatson42, DoctorKubla, Don4of4, Dongemus, Donutz, Doopokko, Dori, Draeco, Drange net, Dreaded Walrus, Dreamyshade, DrewT2, DropDeadGorgias, Dtobias, Dusik, Dxco, EALacey, ERcheck, Ecmsld, EconomicsGuy, Ehurtley, ElKevbo, ElTyrant, Elb2000, Eminence2012, Emj, Enigmar, ErrantX, Error, Eurleif, Evercat, Everyking, Ewald, Exgogogo, Exposay, Extra999, Ezhiki, Family Guy Guy, Fangz, FeralOink, Filzstift, Firsfron, Fiskars007, Fladrif, Flockmeal, Foxj, Fpfp, Frap, Frazzydee, Fredrik, FreplySpang, FrostyBytes, Fruit fig bar, Furrybeagle, Furrykef, FutureDomain, Fuzheado, Fvw, G worroll, GTBacchus, Gamaliel, Gambrills, Gaurav, GentlemanGhost, Geoff43230, Geschichte, Getcrunk, Gettingtoit, Gi Zi Di Ri, Giftlite, Gigs, Gihanuk, Gildir, GirasoleDE, Glane23, Gobonobo, GodNed, Gogobera, Golbez, Goodralph, GossamerBliss, Govtagent82, Gphoto, Gpoduval, Graham87, GrantHenninger, Greatwalk, Greg Tyler, Groink, Gronky, Grunt, Guppie, Gus Polly, Gwendal (usurped), H2g2bob, Hadal, HaeB, Harald Hansen, Helixblue, Hephaestos, Heptapod, Heron, Hongooi, Hoovernj, Hqb, Hurricanefloyd, Huysman, ICEAGE, Ian Moody, Ianb, Ichiroh, Illuminatedwax, InShaneee, Inexplicable, Irishrichy, Isopropyl, Izanbardprince, JForget, JNighthawk, Jacj, Jacob Poon, Jacoplane, Jahilia, Jamdonut, JamesMLane, Jameshales, Janahan, Jannex, Jascha00, Jc iindyysgvxc, Jdavidb, Jearil, JeffAMcGee, Jeffr, Jeremy Visser, JeremyA, Jez9999, Jivecat, Jj137, Jleedev, Jmtaylor90, Jni, JoanneB, Joe chip, Joeinwap, JoelLimberg, Jogers, John254, JohnOwens, JonWinge, Jonathan Williams, JorgeGG, Joy, Jruderman, Jtconroy88, Judzillah, JulesH, JustSomeGuy, Justforasecond, Jwrosenzweig, KBi, Kaaphi, Kadin2048, Kaldari, Karl Meier, Kateshortforbob, Kathleen.wright5, Keithgreer, KelleyCook, Khalid hassani, Khaosworks, Khazar2, Kilo-Lima, Kindall, Klanda, Kniveswood, Knowledge Seeker, Koterpillar, Kpjas, Krakhan, Krisjohn, Kross, Kshieh, Kushieda Minorin, Kv9, Kyz, Larsinio, Leedeth, Leif, Leo Trollstoy, Leviathan, Lexein, Lfwlfw, Liftarn, LiteralKa, Lkgeek, Lobbster, Lod, Loehmann, Loopy48, Looxix, Lopifalko, Lstanley, Lugia2453, Luna Santin, Lupo, Lurker, MBK004, MER-C, Mabdul, Magister Mathematicae, Mahanga, Majumda, Malventano, Marcika, Markaci, Markk97, Markzero, Martarius, MartinHarper, MartinSpamer, MartrtinS, Mat the w, Matt Keleher, MattBowen, Matteh, Matturn, Mav, Maximus Rex, Mblumber, Mboverload, Mecanismo, Meelar, Melaen, Menosofrm, MercuryBlue, Mercurywoodrose, Meshach, Mgunn, Michael Hardy, Michael Snow, Michaelabril, Michaelmas1957, Mike Schwartz, Miles Monroe, Minesweeper, Minghong, Mipadi, Mirv, Misarxist, Mk*, Mkilly, Mm 202, Mo0, Modemac, Mofomojo, Mogism, Morcheeba, Moshe Constantine Hassan Al-Silverburg, Motor, MrJones, Mrzaius, Mscantland, Msikma, MuZemike, Muhgcee, Myanw, N-Man, Nakon, Nanshu, NarQ, Ned Scott, NegroSuave, NeonMerlin, NerdyNSK, Night Gyr, Nightkey, Nil Einne, Njh, Nknight, Nneonneo, Nnp, Nospamme2000, Nova77, Novacatz, Novangelis, Nz17, Obli, Oblivious, Ocolon, Od Mishehu, Ohnoitsjamie, Olivier, OmikronWeapon, Omniscientist, OneNamelessCat, Oscarthecat, OttoMäkelä, Ozzmosis, PReDiToR, Papeschr, Parklandspanaway, Patstuart, Patsw, PaulxSA, Pc13, Pegasus1138, Peter Winnberg, Petrus4, Peyre, PhaseDMA, Phil Sandifer, Philwelch, Plastikspork, Plek, Polarscribe, Ponder, Pretzelpaws, Psantora, Pwnage8, Qbeep, Qcomp, Quaque, Quatloo, Quill E. Coyote, Quinsareth, Quintessent, Quotemstr, Qwerty Binary, R3m0t, Ragib, Random832, Rapidflash, Raul654, Rcsprinter123, Rdsmith4, RedWolf, RedxelaSinnak, Renosan, ReyBrujo, Rhobite, Rich Farmbrough, Richard W.M. Jones, Richi, RickK, Rjwilmsi, Robert K S, RockMFR, Rolloffle, Rorschach, Rossumcapek, Rotten, RuineR, Ryulong, SDNaziWatch, SJP, SMC, SYSS Mouse, Saint bruce, Saint-Paddy, Sam Francis, Sam Korn, Sannse, Sceptre, Schneelocke, Schnell, Schuhpuppe, Schultmc, Sdedeo, Septegram, Serialdogma, Shadok, Shadow1, Shanel, Shentino, ShiningEyes, Sibi antony, Sietse Snel, SigmaEpsilon, Simetrical, SimonP, Simonfrance, Sinalet, SirNuke, Siroxo, Skrates, SkyWalker, Skybon, SlashDot, Sleepyhead81, Sligocki, Slinga, Snori, Soelmese, Solarisworld, Someone is bored at work, Spazik007, Spazztastic, Sphivo, Splash, Spring Rubber, SqueakBox, Squids and Chips, St33lbird, Staticfish, Stephen Gilbert, Stephenb, SteveBaker, StevePR, Stevenj, Stevietheman, Storkk, Straussian, Stw, Sunny256, Sunray, Sweet Rocket, Sysctl, T0ny, Ta bu shi da yu, TakuyaMurata, Tarmas, Tarmle, Tarotcards, Tasc, Tech Nerd, TekNOSX, TerraFrost, Testla, That Guy, From That Show!, The Anome, The Cunctator, The Founders Intent, The Fwanksta, The Inedible Bulk, The Tangent, TheShadowZero, Thecidsound, Thedarxide, Themarcuscreature, Thijs en, Threeafterthree, Thue, Thumperward, Tikiwont, Timetraveller an anthology, Timmie.merc, Timothy Clemans, Tinku99, Titoxd, Tlayn, Tobias Hoevekamp, Toby Douglass, Tomhormby, Tomyumgoong, Tony1, Toph3r, Touro louco, Towel401, Tregoweth, Trevor Bekolay, Trollaxor, Trumpetpunk42, Tt 225, Tumacama, Turrican, Tyomitch, Typhoon, Udonknome, Uncle Dick, Uni4dfx, UnitedStatesian, Uriah923, UserGoogol, Uvulabob27, Vanessaezekowitz, Vbdrummer0, Vcelloho, Vector4F, Vegaswikian, VeryVerily, Violetriga, Vladsinger, Vocaro, Volland, VsA, Vsmith, Wafulz, Walley, Waqas1987, Warreed, Wavelength, Wayne Goode, Wayward, WhisperToMe, Whollabilla, Why me30, Wiki.Tango.Foxtrot, Wikihemos, Will.i.am, Will2k, Wimt, Wonderstruck, Woohookitty, Wrp103, Wwwwolf, WykiP, Xager, Xcentaur, Xnatedawgx, Xneilj, Yagarshitia, YellowMonkey, Yiango, Yoasif, Yomangani, Yonatan, Yooden, ZachPruckowski, Zanderredux, ZeLonewolf, Zoe, Zondor, Zugu, 809 anonymous edits

Denial-of-service_attack *Source*: http://en.wikipedia.org/w/index.php?title=Denial-of-service_attack *Contributors*: A.hawrylyshen, A3 nm, Abgelcartel, Abune, Access Denied, Acdx, Adarw, AdjustShift, Adsf1234, Ahoerstemeier, Alan Taylor, Alanyst, Aldor, Alerante, Alex9788, AlexandrDmitri, Alexius08, Allen4names, AllenZh, Alliekins619, Alphachimp, Ancheta Wis, Anders K Berggren, Andrejj, Andrew Hampe, Andrewpmk, Andrzej P. Wozniak, Andy5421, Aneah, Anetode, Anna Lincoln, Anonauthor, Anonymous Dissident, Antisoft, Apankrat, Ariel@compucall, ArmitageAmy, Armoraid, Arnoldgibson, Artephius, Ashikali1607, Asmeurer, Astt100, Atif.t2, Atif0321, B1atv, Balth3465, Bananastalktome, BanyanTree, Bartledan, Baylink, Beatles2233, Becky Sayles, Beeblebrox, Bemsor, BenTremblay, Berrick, Bgaurav, Bhadani, BigPimpinBrah, Black Falcon, BlackCatN, Blackeagle, Blackmo, Blehfu, Bloodshedder, Blstormo, Bluefoxicy, Bobkeyes, Boborok, Boing! said Zebedee, Bongwarrior, Bradcis, Brento1499, BrianHoef, Brianski, Broadcasterxp, Brusegadi, Bsdlogical, Buck O'Nollege, Bucketsofg, Burfdl, Bushcarrot, Butwhatdoiknow, Bwoodring, CTZMSC3, CWii, Cadence-, CanadianLinuxUser, Canaima, CanisRufus, Carl Turner, Carlo.Ierna, Carlossuarez46, Catamorphism, Cathairawr, Centrx, Charles Matthews, Chengshuotian, Chicken Quiet, Chowbok, Chri$topher, Chris the speller, Christian75, Ciaran H, Cinnamon42, Clapaucius, Clerks, CliffC, Closedmouth, Cmichael, Cogware, Corporal, CosineKitty, Courcelles, Crakkpot, Csabo, Cwagmire, Cyan, CyberSkull, Da31989, Daenney, Danc, DanielPharos, Danny247, Danr2k6, Dark Tea, DarkAudit, DarkMrFrank, Darkfred, Darklord 205, David Fuchs, David Gerard, DavidH, Davken1102, Ddcc, DeadEyeArrow, DeanC81, Deathwiki, Delirium, Delirium of disorder, Deltabeignet, Demiurge1000, Demonkill101, Denisarona, DerHexer, Derek Ross, Deryck Chan, Dicklyon, Discospinster, Dnvrfantj, Donfbreed, Drake144, Drennick, Drogonov, DropDeadGorgias, Drrngrvy, Dsarma, Dschrader, Duzzyman, Dwgould, Dwnd4, Eb1511, Echtner, Echuck215, Ed Poor, Edman274, Eduart.steiner, Egmontaz, Eiler7, ElKevbo, Elecnix, Eliz81, ElizabethFong, Emurphy42, EneMsty12, Equendil, Erianna, Eric-Wester, EricWesBrown, Escheffel, Euclidthalis, Evercat, Everton137, Excirial, Expensivehat, Face, Faheem.pk11, Fang Aili, Fastilysock, Fat&Happy, Favonian, Fedevela, Fffffrrr, Fiddler on the green, Filovirus, FinalRapture, Findepi, Finnish Metal, Fintler, Fireman biff, Flewis, Frankgerlach, Frap, Fredrik, Freekee, Friejose, FrigidNinja, Frosted14, Furrykef, Fuzheado, Gaius Cornelius,

Galassi, Galorr, Gardar Rurak, Gareth Griffith-Jones, Gareth Jones, Gascreed, GateKeeper, Gauss, Gazzat5, Gblaz, Gdm, Geniac, Getmoreatp, Gevron, Ghewgill, Ginsuloft, Gmaxwell, Gmd1722, Goarany, Godzig, Gogo Dodo, GoingBatty, Gomangoman, Goncalopp, Gopher23, Gorman, Goto, Gracefool, GraemeL, Graham87, GreyCat, Gwernol, HMGamerr, HamburgerRadio, Haneef503, HangingCurve, Harry the Dirty Dog, Haseo9999, Henrychan123, Herbythyme, Hmwith, Hu, Hu12, Huds, Hut 8.5, I already forgot, IRP, Iciciliser, Intgr, Irishguy, IsmaelLuceno, Ivan Velikii (2006-2008), Ivhtbr, Ixfd64, J-Baptiste, J.delanoy, JMS Old Al, JOptionPane, JackHenryDyson, Jak32797, Jamesrules90, Janarius, Jaranda, Jarrodmaddy, Jasper Deng, Jcc1, Jcmcc450, Jeannealcid, Jebba, Jesant13, Jhalkompwdr, Jianhui67, Jmoss57, JoanneB, Joefromrandb, Joelee.org, Joemadeus, Joey Eads, Johan Elisson, Johnhax, JonHarder, JonNiola, Jormund, Josh Parris, Josh3580, JoshuaHall155065, Josve05a, Jotag14, Jrmurad, Juanpdp, Julesd, Jwrosenzweig, K. Annoyomous, K7L, KVDP, Kaishen, Kakaopor, Kakurady, Kane5187, Kbdank71, Kbk, Keegen123, Kellyk99, Kenyon, Keraunoscopia, Ketiltrout, Kevo1cat, Kigoe, Kikue26, Killiondude, Kitsunegami, Klaslop, Korath, Kortaggio, KrakatoaKatie, Krellis, Krimanilo, Kristen Eriksen, Kubanczyk, Kuru, Kvng, KyraVixen, LAX, La Parka Your Car, Larrymcp, Lasoraf, Lawandtech, Lawrence Cohen, Ld100, LeaveSleaves, Leemon2010, Lemmio, Life Now, Lightdarkness, Lights, Liko81, LilHelpa, Lionaneesh, Livefastdieold, Liveste, Lloydus98, Looxix, Lothar Kimmeringer, Lotje, Loudsox, Lradrama, Lupo, MC10, MER-C, Maccoat, MadHaTTer666, Madman, Magnus Manske, Magog the Ogre, Mako098765, Malhonen, Mani1, Mann Ltd, Marco Krohn, Marek69, Mark, Mark Arsten, Materialscientist, Matt Casey, Mav, Maximus Rex, Mbell, Mbmexpress, Mboverload, Mchcopl, Mckaysalisbury, Mcnaryxc, Mdupont, MeekMark, MelbourneStar, Melgomac, Melkori, Merlinsorca, Mfordtln, Mgiganteus1, Michael Hardy, Midnightcomm, Mightywayne, Mikaey, Mikeblas, Millisits, Mindmatrix, Minhal Mehdi, Mjdtjm, Mleoking, Mmoneypenny, Modamoda, Monaarora84, Monty845, Mpeg4codec, MrBlueSky, Msamae83, Msick33, Msuzen, Mtcv, Mufka, MugabeeX, Murler, MusikAnimal, Mwikieditor, N-david-l, N3X15, Naniwako, Nbarth, Ncmvocalist, NeoDeGenero, Nethgirb, Neutrality, NicDumZ, Nishkid64, Niteowlneils, NiuWang, Nivix, Nneonneo, No Guru, Nosperantos, NotAnonymous0, Nyttend, O.neill.kid, Ocker3, Oddity-, Oducado, Ogh4x, Ojay123, Olathe, Oliver Lineham, Omicronpersei8, OmidPLuS, One, Op47, Orpenn, Oscar Bravo, Oystein, PPBlais, Pablo Mayrgundter, Paddingtonbaer, Palmbeachguy, Paroxysm, Pastore Italy, Pchachten, Pearle, Pedant17, Peng, Pengo, PentiumMMX, Permalinks, Persian Poet Gal, Peter AUDEMG, Peter Delmonte, Pgr94, Phantomsteve, Philip Trueman, Physicistjedi, PierreAbbat, Plreiher, Pol098, Popo41, Prashanthns, Pwitham, Qrsdogg, QuentinUK, QuiteUnusual, R3m0t, RA0808, RLE64, Racerx11, Raistolo, Ramu50, Randomn1c, Raoravikiran, RattleMan, Raven 1959, Rchamberlain, Rdsmith4, Reacher1989, RedPen, RedWolf, Redvers, RenamedUser01302013, Renoldsmartin, Revolving Bugbear, RexNL, Rfc1394, Rhlitonjua, Rich Farmbrough, RichardMills65, Rjc34, Rjstott, Rjwilmsi, Rm1271, Rmky87, RobLa, Robertvan1, RockMFR, Rofl, Romal, Romeu, Ronhjones, Rosarinjroy, Ross cameron, Rpk74 lb, Rror, Rsrikanth05, Run4health, Ryancarpenter, Ryanmshea, Ryanrs, SaintedLegion, Sam Hocevar, SamSim, Samwb123, Sandgem Addict, Satellizer, Scapler, Scartol, SchnitzelMannGreek, Schnoatbrax, Scientus, Scootey, Sean Whitton, Sephiroth storm, Shaddack, Shadow1, Shadowjams, Shadowlynk, Shaggyjacobs, Shree theultimate, Shuini, Shulini, Shyish, Sid Shadeslayer, Sierra 1, Signalhead, Silas S. Brown, Silversam, Skiidoo, SkyWalker, Slakr, Sligocki, Smalljim, Smallman12q, Sngs87, Snowolf, Softwaredude, SoledadKabocha, Soma mishra, SonicAD, Sophus Bie, SoulSkorpion, Spaceman85, Sparky132, Spartytime, Splintercellguy, Starkiller88, Stephenchou0722, StewE17, Stogers, Stphnm, Streakydjl, Strike Eagle, Stultiwikia, Sunholm, Sunndil, SuperHamster, Swearwolf666, Synchronism, T23c, THEN WHO WAS PHONE?, TT-97976, TakaGA, Taxman, Tckma, Team Blitz, Teapeat, Teknopup, Tempshill, Tentinator, Terryr rodery, The Anome, The Cute Philosopher, TheMightyOrb, Thewrite1, Thexelt, Tide rolls, Timwi, Titi 3bood, Tmaufer, TonyJunak, Toobulkeh, Totakeke423, Tothwolf, Tragic8, Tree Biting Conspiracy, Trigguh, Trivialist, Tuspm, TyA, Ulric1313, Ultimus, Uncle Dick, UnitedStatesian, Unschool, Usbdriver, Useight, VKokielov, Vashtihorvat, Vedge, Vegardw, Velella, VernoWhitney, Vicarious, Victor, Vinsanity123, Violetriga, ViperSnake151, Viperdeck PyTh0n, Vlhsrp, W.F.Galway, WAS 4.250, WadeSimMiser, Walshga, Warrush, Wayward, WeatherFug, Web-Crawling Stickler, Webhostingtips, Wesha, WhisperToMe, White Ash, Who, Whsazdfhnbfxgnh, Widr, WikHead, Wikfr, Wikibert, Wikimol, William Ortiz, Wiredsoul, Wjejskenewr, Wmahan, Wolfkeeper, Woody, Woohookitty, Worldnewsinformant, Wragge, Writ Keeper, Wrs1864, Xavier6984, Xawieri, Xee, Xionbox, Xiphiidae, Xitrax, XtAzY, Yaltaplace, Yehaah, Yonatan, Yooden, Yudiweb, Zabanio, Zac439, Zedmelon, Zhangyongmei, Zhouf12, Zsinj, Zzsql, Île flottante, Սահակ, לורם מ׳אפר, 1505 anonymous edits

Image Sources, Licenses and Contributors

File:MUD1 screenshot.gif *Source*: http://en.wikipedia.org/w/index.php?title=File:MUD1_screenshot.gif *License*: unknown *Contributors*: Skier Dude, Trlkly

Image:evemarketscreen.png *Source*: http://en.wikipedia.org/w/index.php?title=File:Evemarketscreen.png *License*: unknown *Contributors*: 6birc, Beefnut, Ghosttr, Melesse, Rockfang

Image:UOPlayerInteraction.jpg *Source*: http://en.wikipedia.org/w/index.php?title=File:UOPlayerInteraction.jpg *License*: unknown *Contributors*: Abu badali, Beefnut, CountingPine, Hu12, Instinct, Ixfd64, Kx1186, MaXiMiUS, Mahahahaneapneap, Mormegil, Paxse, Porqin, Rhobite, Shanes, Skier Dude, SmileToday, The Thing That Should Not Be, The Yar, Webclient101, 41 anonymous edits

Image:Sand Giant - EverQuest - 1999.jpg *Source*: http://en.wikipedia.org/w/index.php?title=File:Sand_Giant_-_EverQuest_-_1999.jpg *License*: unknown *Contributors*: Chaos5023, N. Harmonik, Vranak

File:Nasdaq2.png *Source*: http://en.wikipedia.org/w/index.php?title=File:Nasdaq2.png *License*: unknown *Contributors*: User:Little Professor

Image:Slashdot omgponies.png *Source*: http://en.wikipedia.org/w/index.php?title=File:Slashdot_omgponies.png *License*: unknown *Contributors*: User:Wiki.Tango.Foxtrot

File:Rob 'CmdrTaco' Malda crop.jpeg *Source*: http://en.wikipedia.org/w/index.php?title=File:Rob_'CmdrTaco'_Malda_crop.jpeg *License*: unknown *Contributors*: Jared and Corin

File:Tux.svg *Source*: http://en.wikipedia.org/w/index.php?title=File:Tux.svg *License*: unknown *Contributors*: Larry Ewing, Simon Budig, Anja Gerwinski

File:Stachledraht DDos Attack.svg *Source*: http://en.wikipedia.org/w/index.php?title=File:Stachledraht_DDos_Attack.svg *License*: unknown *Contributors*: Everaldo Coelho and YellowIcon

NU Free Documentation License Version 1.2, ovember 2002 Copyright (C) 2000,2001,2002 ree Software Foundation, Inc. 59 Temple lace, Suite 330, Boston, MA 02111-1307 USA veryone is permitted to copy and distribute erbatim copies of this license document, but hanging it is not allowed.

PREAMBLE

he purpose of this License is to make a manual, textbook, or her functional and useful document "free" in the sense of eedom: to assure everyone the effective freedom to copy and distribute it, with or without modifying it, either commercially or ncommercially. Secondarily, this License preserves for the thor and publisher a way to get credit for their work, while not ing considered responsible for modifications made by others. is License is a kind of "copyleft", which means that derivative orks of the document must themselves be free in the same nse. It complements the GNU General Public License, which is copyleft license designed for free software. We have designed s License in order to use it for manuals for free software, ecause free software needs free documentation: a free program ould come with manuals providing the same freedoms that the ftware does. But this License is not limited to software manuals; can be used for any textual work, regardless of subject matter whether it is published as a printed book. We recommend this cense principally for works whose purpose is instruction or ference.

APPLICABILITY AND DEFINITIONS

his License applies to any manual or other work, in any edium, that contains a notice placed by the copyright holder aying it can be distributed under the terms of this License. Such notice grants a world-wide, royalty-free license, unlimited in iration, to use that work under the conditions stated herein. The Document", below, refers to any such manual or work. Any ember of the public is a licensee, and is addressed as "you". ou accept the license if you copy, modify or distribute the work a way requiring permission under copyright law. A "Modified ersion" of the Document means any work containing the ocument or a portion of it, either copied verbatim, or with odifications and/or translated into another language. A Secondary Section" is a named appendix or a front-matter ection of the Document that deals exclusively with the lationship of the publishers or authors of the Document to the ocument's overall subject (or to related matters) and contains othing that could fall directly within that overall subject. (Thus, if e Document is in part a textbook of mathematics, a Secondary ection may not explain any mathematics.) The relationship could e a matter of historical connection with the subject or with elated matters, or of legal, commercial, philosophical, ethical or olitical position regarding them. The "Invariant Sections" are ertain Secondary Sections whose titles are designated, as being ose of Invariant Sections, in the notice that says that the ocument is released under this License. If a section does not fit e above definition of Secondary then it is not allowed to be esignated as Invariant. The Document may contain zero nvariant Sections. If the Document does not identify any Invariant ections then there are none. The "Cover Texts" are certain short assages of text that are listed, as Front-Cover Texts or Back-Cover Texts, in the notice that says that the Document is eleased under this License. A Front-Cover Text may be at most words, and a Back-Cover Text may be at most 25 words. A Transparent" copy of the Document means a machine-readable opy, represented in a format whose specification is available to e general public, that is suitable for revising the document traightforwardly with generic text editors or (for images omposed of pixels) generic paint programs or (for drawings) ome widely available drawing editor, and that is suitable for input text formatters or for automatic translation to a variety of ormats suitable for input to text formatters. A copy made in an therwise Transparent file format whose markup, or absence of narkup, has been arranged to thwart or discourage subsequent nodification by readers is not Transparent. An image format is ot Transparent if used for any substantial amount of text. A copy hat is not "Transparent" is called "Opaque". Examples of suitable ormats for Transparent copies include plain ASCII without narkup, Texinfo input format, LaTeX input format, SGML or XML sing a publicly available DTD, and standard-conforming simple HTML, PostScript or PDF designed for human modification. Examples of transparent image formats include PNG, XCF and JPG. Opaque formats include proprietary formats that can be ead and edited only by proprietary word processors, SGML or XML for which the DTD and/or processing tools are not generally available, and the machine-generated HTML, PostScript or PDF produced by some word processors for output purposes only. The Title Page" means, for a printed book, the title page itself, plus such following pages as are needed to hold, legibly, the material his License requires to appear in the title page. For works in ormats which do not have any title page as such, "Title Page" neans the text near the most prominent appearance of the work's itle, preceding the beginning of the body of the text. A section Entitled XYZ" means a named subunit of the Document whose itle either is precisely XYZ or contains XYZ in parentheses ollowing text that translates XYZ in another language. (Here XYZ stands for a specific section name mentioned below, such as "Acknowledgements", "Dedications", "Endorsements", or "History".) To "Preserve the Title" of such a section when you nodify the Document means that it remains a section "Entitled XYZ" according to this definition. The Document may include Warranty Disclaimers next to the notice which states that this License applies to the Document. These Warranty Disclaimers are considered to be included by reference in this License, but only as regards disclaiming warranties: any other implication that these Warranty Disclaimers may have is void and has no effect on the meaning of this License.

2. VERBATIM COPYING

You may copy and distribute the Document in any medium, either commercially or noncommercially, provided that this License, the copyright notices, and the license notice saying this License applies to the Document are reproduced in all copies, and that you add no other conditions whatsoever to those of this License. You may not use technical measures to obstruct or control the reading or further copying of the copies you make or distribute. However, you may accept compensation in exchange for copies. If you distribute a large enough number of copies you must also follow the conditions in section 3. You may also lend copies, under the same conditions stated above, and you may publicly display copies.

3. COPYING IN QUANTITY

If you publish printed copies (or copies in media that commonly have printed covers) of the Document, numbering more than 100, and the Document's license notice requires Cover Texts, you must enclose the copies in covers that carry, clearly and legibly, all these Cover Texts: Front-Cover Texts on the front cover, and Back-Cover Texts on the back cover. Both covers must also clearly and legibly identify you as the publisher of these copies. The front cover must present the full title with all words of the title equally prominent and visible. You may add other material on the covers in addition. Copying with changes limited to the covers, as long as they preserve the title of the Document and satisfy these conditions, can be treated as verbatim copying in other respects. If the required texts for either cover are too voluminous to fit legibly, you should put the first ones listed (as many as fit reasonably) on the actual cover, and continue the rest onto adjacent pages. If you publish or distribute Opaque copies of the Document numbering more than 100, you must either include a machine-readable Transparent copy along with each Opaque copy, or state in or with each Opaque copy a computer-network location from which the general network-using public has access to download using public-standard network protocols a complete Transparent copy of the Document, free of added material. If you use the latter option, you must take reasonably prudent steps, when you begin distribution of Opaque copies in quantity, to ensure that this Transparent copy will remain thus accessible at the stated location until at least one year after the last time you distribute an Opaque copy (directly or through your agents or retailers) of that edition to the public. It is requested, but not required, that you contact the authors of the Document well before redistributing any large number of copies, to give them a chance to provide you with an updated version of the Document.

4. MODIFICATIONS

You may copy and distribute a Modified Version of the Document under the conditions of sections 2 and 3 above, provided that you release the Modified Version under precisely this License, with the Modified Version filling the role of the Document, thus licensing distribution and modification of the Modified Version to whoever possesses a copy of it. In addition, you must do these things in the Modified Version: A. Use in the Title Page (and on the covers, if any) a title distinct from that of the Document, and from those of previous versions (which should, if there were any, be listed in the History section of the Document). You may use the same title as a previous version if the original publisher of that version gives permission. B. List on the Title Page, as authors, one or more persons or entities responsible for authorship of the modifications in the Modified Version, together with at least five of the principal authors of the Document (all of its principal authors, if it has fewer than five), unless they release you from this requirement. C. State on the Title page the name of the publisher of the Modified Version, as the publisher. D. Preserve all the copyright notices of the Document. E. Add an appropriate copyright notice for your modifications adjacent to the other copyright notices. F. Include, immediately after the copyright notices, a license notice giving the public permission to use the Modified Version under the terms of this License, in the form shown in the Addendum below. G. Preserve in that license notice the full lists of Invariant Sections and required Cover Texts given in the Document's license notice. H. Include an unaltered copy of this License. I. Preserve the section Entitled "History", Preserve its Title, and add to it an item stating at least the title, year, new authors, and publisher of the Modified Version as given on the Title Page. If there is no section Entitled "History" in the Document, create one stating the title, year, authors, and publisher of the Document as given on its Title Page, then add an item describing the Modified Version as stated in the previous sentence. J. Preserve the network location, if any, given in the Document for public access to a Transparent copy of the Document, and likewise the network locations given in the Document for previous versions it was based on. These may be placed in the "History" section. You may omit a network location for a work that was published at least four years before the Document itself, or if the original publisher of the version it refers to gives permission. K. For any section Entitled "Acknowledgements" or "Dedications", Preserve the Title of the section, and preserve in the section all the substance and tone of each of the contributor acknowledgements and/or dedications given therein. L. Preserve all the Invariant Sections of the Document, unaltered in their text and in their titles. Section numbers or the equivalent are not considered part of the section titles. M. Delete any section Entitled "Endorsements". Such a section may not be included in the Modified Version. N. Do not retitle any existing section to be Entitled "Endorsements" or to conflict in title with any Invariant Section. O. Preserve any Warranty Disclaimers. If the Modified Version includes new front-matter sections or appendices that qualify as Secondary Sections and contain no material copied from the Document, you may at your option designate some or all of these sections as invariant. To do this, add their titles to the list of Invariant Sections in the Modified Version's license notice. These titles must be distinct from any other section titles. You may add a section Entitled "Endorsements", provided it contains nothing but endorsements of your Modified Version by various parties--for example, statements of peer review or that the text has been approved by an organization as the authoritative definition of a standard. You may add a passage of up to five words as a Front-Cover Text, and a passage of up to 25 words as a Back-Cover Text, to the end of the list of Cover Texts in the Modified Version. Only one passage of Front-Cover Text and one of Back-Cover Text may be added by (or through arrangements made by) any one entity. If the Document already includes a cover text for the same cover, previously added by you or by arrangement made by the same entity you are acting on behalf of, you may not add another; but you may replace the old one, on explicit permission from the previous publisher that added the old one. The author(s) and publisher(s) of the Document do not by this License give permission to use their names for publicity for or to assert or imply endorsement of any Modified Version.

5. COMBINING DOCUMENTS

You may combine the Document with other documents released under this License, under the terms defined in section 4 above for modified versions, provided that you include in the combination all of the Invariant Sections of all of the original documents, unmodified, and list them all as Invariant Sections of your combined work in its license notice, and that you preserve all their Warranty Disclaimers. The combined work need only contain one copy of this License, and multiple identical Invariant Sections may be replaced with a single copy. If there are multiple Invariant Sections with the same name but different contents, make the title of each such section unique by adding at the end of it, in parentheses, the name of the original author or publisher of that section if known, or else a unique number. Make the same adjustment to the section titles in the list of Invariant Sections in the license notice of the combined work. In the combination, you must combine any sections Entitled "History" in the various original documents, forming one section Entitled "History"; likewise combine any sections Entitled "Acknowledgements", and any sections Entitled "Dedications". You must delete all sections Entitled "Endorsements".

6. COLLECTIONS OF DOCUMENTS

You may make a collection consisting of the Document and other documents released under this License, and replace the individual copies of this License in the various documents with a single copy that is included in the collection, provided that you follow the rules of this License for verbatim copying of each of the documents in all other respects. You may extract a single document from such a collection, and distribute it individually under this License, provided you insert a copy of this License into the extracted document, and follow this License in all other respects regarding verbatim copying of that document.

7. AGGREGATION WITH INDEPENDENT WORKS

A compilation of the Document or its derivatives with other separate and independent documents or works, in or on a volume of a storage or distribution medium, is called an "aggregate" if the copyright resulting from the compilation is not used to limit the legal rights of the compilation's users beyond what the individual works permit. When the Document is included in an aggregate, this License does not apply to the other works in the aggregate which are not themselves derivative works of the Document. If the Cover Text requirement of section 3 is applicable to these copies of the Document, then if the Document is less than one half of the entire aggregate, the Document's Cover Texts may be placed on covers that bracket the Document within the aggregate, or the electronic equivalent of covers if the Document is in electronic form. Otherwise they must appear on printed covers that bracket the whole aggregate.

8. TRANSLATION

Translation is considered a kind of modification, so you may distribute translations of the Document under the terms of section 4. Replacing Invariant Sections with translations requires special permission from their copyright holders, but you may include translations of some or all Invariant Sections in addition to the original versions of these Invariant Sections. You may include a translation of this License, and all the license notices in the Document, and any Warranty Disclaimers, provided that you also include the original English version of this License and the original versions of those notices and disclaimers. In case of a disagreement between the translation and the original version of this License or a notice or disclaimer, the original version will prevail. If a section in the Document is Entitled "Acknowledgements", "Dedications", or "History", the requirement (section 4) to Preserve its Title (section 1) will typically require changing the actual title.

9. TERMINATION

You may not copy, modify, sublicense, or distribute the Document except as expressly provided for under this License. Any other attempt to copy, modify, sublicense or distribute the Document is void, and will automatically terminate your rights under this License. However, parties who have received copies, or rights, from you under this License will not have their licenses terminated so long as such parties remain in full compliance.

10. FUTURE REVISIONS OF THIS LICENSE

The Free Software Foundation may publish new, revised versions of the GNU Free Documentation License from time to time. Such new versions will be similar in spirit to the present version, but may differ in detail to address new problems or concerns. See http://www.gnu.org/copyleft/. Each version of the License is given a distinguishing version number. If the Document specifies that a particular numbered version of this License "or any later version" applies to it, you have the option of following the terms and conditions either of that specified version or of any later version that has been published (not as a draft) by the Free Software Foundation. If the Document does not specify a version number of this License, you may choose any version ever published (not as a draft) by the Free Software Foundation. ADDENDUM: How to use this License for your documents To use this License in a document you have written, include a copy of the License in the document and put the following copyright and license notices just after the title page: Copyright (c) YEAR YOUR NAME. Permission is granted to copy, distribute and/or modify this document under the terms of the GNU Free Documentation License, Version 1.2 or any later version published by the Free Software Foundation; with no Invariant Sections, no Front-Cover Texts, and no Back-Cover Texts. A copy of the license is included in the section entitled "GNU Free Documentation License". If you have Invariant Sections, Front-Cover Texts and Back-Cover Texts, replace the "with...Texts." line with this: with the Invariant Sections being LIST THEIR TITLES, with the Front-Cover Texts being LIST, and with the Back-Cover Texts being LIST. If you have Invariant Sections without Cover Texts, or some other combination of the three, merge those two alternatives to suit the situation. If your document contains nontrivial examples of program code, we recommend releasing these examples in parallel under your choice of free software license, such as the GNU General Public License, to permit their use in free software.

MIX
Papier aus verantwortungsvollen Quellen
Paper from responsible sources
FSC® C105338

Printed by Books on Demand GmbH, Norderstedt / Germany